# INSECTS
## OF SOUTH AFRICA

MIKE PICKER & CHARLES GRIFFITHS

Published by Struik Nature
(an imprint of Penguin Random House South Africa (Pty) Ltd)
Reg. No. 1953/000441/07
The Estuaries No 4, Oxbow Crescent,
Century Avenue, Century City, 7441
PO Box 1144, Cape Town, 8000 South Africa

Visit **www.randomstruik.co.za** and join the Struik Nature Club
for updates, news, events and special offers.

1 3 5 7 9 10 8 6 4 2

Copyright © in text, 2015: Charles Griffiths and Mike Picker
Copyright © in photographs, 2015: Charles Griffiths and Mike Picker,
except where otherwise indicated
Copyright © in maps, 2015: Charles Griffiths and Mike Picker
Copyright © in published edition, 2015: Penguin
Random House South Africa (Pty) Ltd

Publisher: Pippa Parker
Managing editor: Helen de Villiers
Editor: Emily Bowles
Design team: Gillian Black and Neil Bester

Reproduction by Hirt & Carter Cape (Pty) Ltd
Printed and bound by Times Offset (M) Sdn Bhd, Malaysia

All rights reserved. No part of this publication may be reproduced, stored in a retrieval system, or transmitted, in any form or by any means, electronic, mechanical, photocopying, recording or otherwise, without the prior written permission of the copyright owner(s).

Print: 978 1 77584 195 1
ePub: 978 1 77584 197 5
ePDF: 978 1 77584 196 8

Front cover: Rainbow shield bug, *Calidea dregii* (Ernita van Wyk)
Back cover, top to bottom: Parktown prawn, *Libanasidus vittatus*;
Striped toktokkie, *Psammodes striatus*; cuckoo wasp, *Chrysis concinna*;
dobsonfly larvae, *Taeniochauliodes ochraceopennis*
Page 1: Roseate emperor moth, *Eochroa trimenii*
Contents page, top to bottom: Brush jewel beetle, *Julodis* sp.;
Lunate ladybird, *Cheilomenes lunata*; Luna moth, *Argema mimosae*;
Red-spotted spittle bug, *Locris arithmetica*

## ACKNOWLEDGEMENTS

This book would not have been possible without the help of Emily Djock, who sorted out the necessary images and maps. We are also grateful to the various photographers who kindly allowed us to make use of their images, as credited. Lastly, our thanks to Emily Bowles, Gillian Black and Neil Bester for their meticulous editing and design of the book.

# CONTENTS

## Introduction 4
Insect body parts 5
Insect life cycles 6
Importance of insects 7
Where to find insects 10
How to use this book 11

## Species accounts 12
Springtails: Collembola 12
Diplurans: Diplura 12
Silverfish: Thysanura 13
Bristletails: Archaeognatha 13
Mayflies: Ephemeroptera 14
Damselflies and dragonflies: Odonata 16
Cockroaches: Blattodea 21
Termites: Isoptera 24
Mantids: Mantodea 26
Earwigs: Dermaptera 30
Stoneflies: Plecoptera 31
Crickets, katydids, grasshoppers
 and locusts: Orthoptera 32
Webspinners: Embiidina (Embioptera) 42
Heelwalkers: Mantophasmatodea 43
Stick insects: Phasmatodea 44
Psocids (Booklice): Psocoptera 45
Lice: Phthiraptera 46
Bugs: Hemiptera 47
Thrips: Thysanoptera 61
Dobsonflies and alderflies: Megaloptera 62
Antlions and lacewings: Neuroptera 63
Beetles: Coleoptera 66
Twisted wing parasites: Strepsiptera 88
Hangingflies and scorpion flies: Mecoptera 88
Flies: Diptera 89
Fleas: Siphonaptera 105
Caddisflies: Trichoptera 106
Moths and butterflies: Lepidoptera 107
Sawflies, wasps, bees and ants:
 Hymenoptera 129

## Glossary 141
## Further reading 142
## Index to scientific names 142
## Index to common names 148

# INTRODUCTION

What is an insect? Insects are a class of animals within a larger group – the phylum Arthropoda – that includes all animals with jointed external skeletons. Arthropods are easily the most diverse animal group, making up 90% of all animal species and dominating most marine, freshwater and terrestrial habitats.

Among the many arthropod groups, insects are the only ones to have developed wings. Other features that identify insects are: the division of the body into 3 obvious sections, head, thorax and abdomen, and the possession of 3 pairs of legs and a single pair of antennae. Insects are by far the most diverse arthropod group. Other major arthropod groups potentially confused with insects include the following:

**SPIDERS** have 4 pairs of legs, no antennae and a body comprised of 2 sections – a fused head and thorax separated by a narrow 'waist' from an unsegmented abdomen. They are well known for their ability to spin silk webs, snares and shelters. All are predatory and a few species are dangerously venomous.

A fishing spider (family Pisauridae) hunts on water.

**SCORPIONS** lack antennae and have 4 pairs of walking legs and another pair of legs that form powerful pincers.

The thick-tailed scorpion *Parabuthus villosus* is dangerously venomous.

The head and thorax are fused, and the elongated, segmented abdomen ends in a distinctive swollen sting. Scorpions are nocturnal predators and some are dangerously venomous.

**MYRIOPODS** (centipedes and millipedes) are easily distinguished from insects by their elongate body form, multiple body segments and lack of separation between thorax and abdomen. Legs are present on all body segments except the head. Centipedes are generally flattened and have 1 pair of legs per body segment, while millipedes are usually cylindrical with 2 pairs of legs per segment. Large centipedes can inflict a painful, venomous bite.

The *Chersastus* millipede has distinctive warning coloration.

**CRUSTACEANS** (crabs, woodlice and landhoppers) have 2 pairs of antennae and a variable number of legs. They are much more significant than insects in marine systems, but are less common in freshwater and terrestrial ecosystems. Crabs have a fused head and thorax and 5 pairs of legs, the first pair modified into pincers. Woodlice and landhoppers have 7 thoracic segments and pairs of legs (the first 1 or 2 sometimes modified into pincers). Woodlice are flattened (depressed), with short legs, while landhoppers are flattened from side to side (compressed), with longer jumping legs.

The introduced woodlouse *Porcellio scaber*; note the flattened body and multiple body segments.

## INSECT BODY PARTS

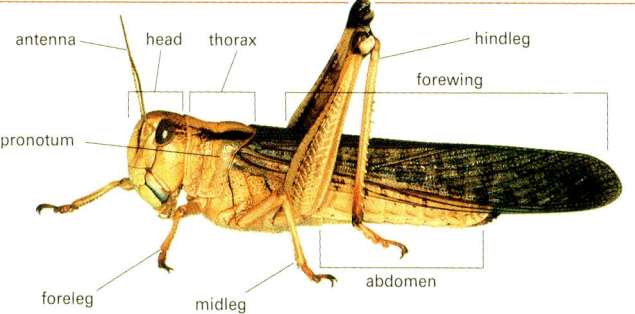

The anatomy of a grasshopper

The bodies of adult insects are encased in a hard exoskeleton made up of separate plates ('sclerites'), joined together by flexible sections ('pleurites') that allow for movement, much like a suit of armour. As already mentioned, there are 3 main body sections: head, thorax and abdomen.

The **head** is made up of 6 fused segments and carries:
- jointed **antennae**, a single pair, of variable length and structure;
- **eyes**, usually prominent compound eyes composed of numerous independent sensory structures ('ommatidea'), visible externally as hexagonal facets, but often also small simple eyes ('ocelli') between the compound eyes; and
- **mouthparts** of enormously variable structure.

The basic chewing or biting mouthparts can be modified into elongate, tubular, piercing-and-sucking structures (in bugs and mosquitoes), an elongate, coiled proboscis for nectar-feeding (in butterflies and moths), or a blunt suction pad to mop up liquids (in flies).

Bugs (Hemiptera) are easily recognized by their elongate piercing-and-sucking mouthparts.

**INTRODUCTION** 5

The **thorax** is composed of 3 segments (the pro-, meso- and metathorax), each bearing:

- **legs**, 1 pair per segment: the first 2 segments of each leg are small and the large 'thigh' or femur is the third segment, followed by the long, thin tibia and a 5-segmented foot or 'tarsus', the last segment of which often bears sharp claws; and
- **wings**, usually 2 pairs, but these may be absent, especially in primitive and parasitic groups; they may also be variously modified in other groups, for example the forewings of beetles are modified into protective covers ('elytra'), while the hindwings of flies are modified into small balancing organs ('halteres').

The **abdomen** usually consists of 11 relatively soft segments and contains most of the digestive and reproductive organs. Usually the only appendages are the terminal

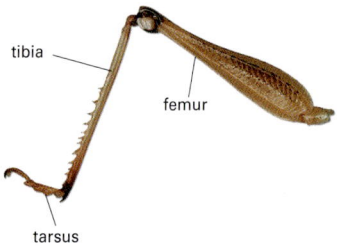

Leg of a locust showing the 3 major segments: femur, tibia and tarsus.

egg-laying tube ('ovipositor') in females, which can be very long and conspicuous, and the more complicated copulatory structures of males, used to stabilize the female's abdomen during mating. In some groups, long segmented pincers ('cerci') may be present at the end of the abdomen. Small pores ('spiracles') opening into the respiratory system may be visible on the side of each segment.

## INSECT LIFE CYCLES

Because their bodies are covered by a rigid exoskeleton, insects can grow only by periodically shedding their skins ('moulting'). During the moulting process the hard outer skin is discarded, allowing a new, soft one beneath it to expand and then harden. Growth is thus not continuous, but takes place in a series of discrete steps. Each growth stage is termed an 'instar' and most insects go though 4–8 instars during their life cycles. Normally, it is only the last adult instar that is capable of reproduction and flight.

Adult insects, apart from the most primitive, the fish moths, never grow. The adult size of each insect species is thus consistent and is a good identification feature, although there may be some variation in size, attributable to differences in food availability during development.

The life histories of insects follow one of two patterns. In more primitive groups, eggs hatch into nymphs that resemble tiny wingless adults and that tend to live in the same habitat and eat the same food as adults. As the nymphs develop and grow, these later instars develop wing buds, which become functional wings only after the last moult into the adult. Such insects are termed 'hemimetabolous' (*hemi* = 'half', *metabolos* = 'changeable'), and they include grasshoppers, mantids, cockroaches and bugs.

In other, more advanced, groups of insects, such as butterflies, beetles and flies, the egg hatches into a larva, which is completely unlike the adult in appearance and habitat and

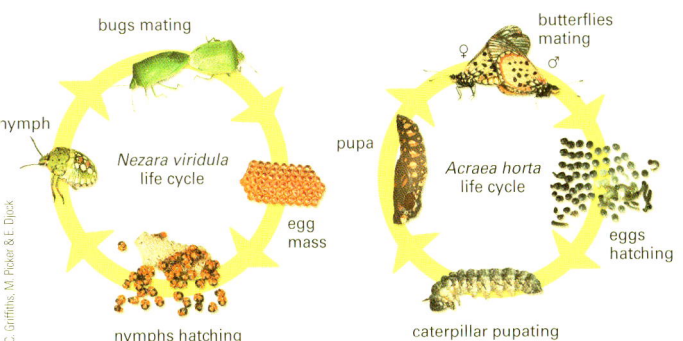

Life cycle of a Green stinkbug *Nezara viridula* (left) and that of a Garden acraea butterfly *Acraea horta* (right).

usually exploits quite different food resources from the adult. The larva grows though a number of instars before entering an immobile pupal stage in which the entire body is restructured into the (usually) winged adult. Such a life history is termed 'holometabolous' (*holo* = 'entire', *metabolos* = 'changeable'). These two patterns are illustrated above, as exemplified by a hemimetabolous bug and holometabolous butterfly.

## IMPORTANCE OF INSECTS

There are more species of insect than of any other group of organisms on the planet – over 1 million different species have been described, and it is estimated that there are an additional 3–30 million species awaiting discovery and description. As recently as 2002 a new insect order, Mantophasmatodea (p.43), was discovered in southern Africa. This is equivalent to discovering bats, primates or whales among the mammals for the first time.

Mantophasmatodea (*Karoophasma* sp. shown, mating) is a newly discovered insect order.

INTRODUCTION

Insects occupy every habitat possible, including almost boiling hot springs and subantarctic islands. Fewer species, however, exist in the oceans or in polar regions. The insects are not only very rich in species, their numbers (and biomass) can also be very great, and for this reason they form a major component of food webs in both terrestrial and aquatic habitats.

Many animals, particularly smaller mammals, birds and reptiles, depend heavily or entirely on insects for food. Indeed, even among insects themselves there are many species that either predate on or parasitize other insects and thus play a prominent role in regulating the numbers of herbivorous insects that would otherwise cause extensive defoliation and crop losses.

Since insect bodies contain very high levels of protein and fat, they also comprise a valuable food resource for humans in many non-industrialized countries, especially those in Africa and Asia. In Botswana and other parts of southern Africa, Mopane worms *Imbrasia belina* (p.118) provide a protein source for millions and also form the basis of a lucrative export industry. Their very high protein content (64% of their dry weight) makes them a better source of protein than beef, chicken or fish. In certain parts of Africa millions of people are reliant on additional insect species – these include *Macrotermes* termites (p.25), migratory locusts (p.32) and many other grasshopper species, as well as various bugs, the Hemiptera (p.47). Honey is a staple in most countries, and although generally collected from honeybee colonies, it is also collected from smaller native bees. In the East, silkworms *Bombyx mori* have traditionally been used to produce silk. The cochineal bug *Dactylopius coccus* produces carminic acid, the red dye used to make carmine, which is responsible for the crimson colour in lipstick and many foods.

Almost all crop plants require insect pollinators, and the honeybee *Apis mellifera* (p.137) does most of

The Acacia gall wasp *Trichilogaster acaciaelongifoliae* reduces the seed bank of the invasive Long-leafed wattle *Acacia longifolia* by galling the flower buds and preventing seed production.

**INTRODUCTION**

the work. However, native pollinators also play an important role in areas where honeybee populations are low, or pollination requires specialized pollinators. Native pollinators in undisturbed tracts of land adjacent to crops play an important role in crop pollination, hence the need to conserve natural ecosystems in the vicinity of agricultural lands. There are many other beneficial insects, most of which are predators or parasites that regulate the numbers of plant-feeding insects. Insects are also very widely used as biological control agents to contain the spread of alien plants. Typically, seed-feeding insects are sourced from the weed's country of origin and, after stringent trials, are released into areas containing invasive alien plants. They are effective in reducing the quantity of seed produced and can thus slow down the spread of alien plants – in some cases even eliminating the plants entirely.

Insects consume an estimated 20% of all global agricultural production. During the domestication

## PUSH-PULL PEST MANAGEMENT

The innovative 'push-pull agricultural pest management' programme relies on natural ecosystem processes to protect maize and other cereal crops from destructive stem-boring moths. Small plants producing repellent substances are interplanted among maize plants to 'push' these moths away from the maize plants. At the same time, native and alien grasses that are suitable host plants for stem borers are planted around the maize field, thus attracting ('pulling') the moths away from the maize. The result is an effective natural system with very low levels of infestation of maize plants and one that obviates the need for any application of pesticides.

of food plants, many of the defence mechanisms of these crops were lost through selective breeding for high yields. In addition, farmers generally plant crops as a monoculture, enabling insect species that feed on a particular crop to build up very large populations. The use of pesticides kills off all the natural predators and parasitoids (insects that parasitize other insects) of the crop-feeding insects.

Although only about 0.5% of all insects can be considered pests or pathogens, even a few species can wreak havoc with human and animal health because of their abundance and ability to move across large areas. For example, the tsetse fly *Glossina morsitans* (p.102), which transmits the protozoan disease leishmaniasis, is estimated to affect 100 million humans and 60 million cattle in Africa. Malaria in Africa accounts for about 0.5 million deaths per annum, with over 200 million infections annually. As with sleeping sickness and many other serious human diseases in Africa, blood-sucking flies are the vectors.

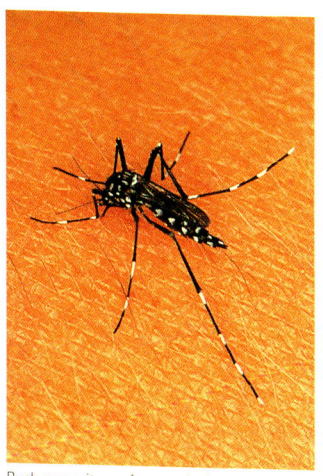

Bush mosquitoes of genus *Aedes* are important vectors of yellow fever and elephantiasis.

INTRODUCTION

# WHERE TO FIND INSECTS

Since insects are generally small and very numerous, they can be found in virtually every habitat, no matter how tiny. Even a suburban garden has a rich and complex community of both native and alien insects. The air is filled with small and large flying insects; many more occur on vegetation; others are found under rocks, bark, logs or in the soil, while even aquatic habitats have their own rich and distinctive insect communities.

Insects are attracted to lights emitting short wavelengths.

Observations of insects are improved with the use of a 10x hand lens (a jeweller's loupe or folding hand lens). A very wide assortment of spectacular insects can be observed while walking through natural habitats in South Africa – although most insects are hidden much of the time and can be detected only by means of specialized collecting methods. In the winter-rainfall region, the best time to look for insects is in spring and early summer, when flowers are abundant. In the summer-rainfall parts of the country, insect life is most abundant some time after the first rains, generally in midsummer.

A huge variety of otherwise rarely seen insects are attracted to lights on warm, wind-free evenings. More are attracted to ultraviolet lights, which can be hung in front of a white sheet or against a light-coloured wall.

The adults of aquatic insects generally remain in close proximity to the water body where their larvae develop. Adult dragonflies, damselflies, caddisflies and stoneflies all occur on rocks, plants and the branches of vegetation bordering water bodies. Their presence can often be detected by observing nymphal skins ('shucks') adhering to reeds, rocks or logs protruding above the water surface. The nymphs can be found by turning over rocks and stones in streams, or they can be strained from water plants using a stout net.

Terrestrial insects often concentrate on flowers. This includes both pollinators and their predators, such as assassin bugs and flower mantids. Native trees in flower can attract an impressive variety of pollen feeders and predators, and it is particularly worthwhile having a closer look at flowering karees, *Searsia* spp., buffalo thorns, *Zizyphus* spp., raisinberries, *Grewia* spp., and acacias, *Vachellia* spp.

This is the shuck left by a stonefly nymph that has moulted; note the tracheal breathing tubes. Dragonflies and caddisflies also leave shucks.

# HOW TO USE THIS BOOK

This guide covers some of the more common and interesting insects of the region. As only a fraction of the 100,000-odd South African species can be dealt with, many of the entries have been written at the family level. Thus it might not always be possible to identify a particular insect to species using this guide, but since most members of a particular insect family are similar in appearance, behaviour and ecology, it should be possible to identify it to family level.

❶ The structure of the book uses the **order** (a high-level classification category) as the starting point for each new section, e.g. order Coleoptera (beetles). The next classification level – the **family** – follows. At least one family representative has been shown for each of the families covered.

❷ For each entry (whether family, genus or species) a **distribution map** is provided. These maps refer to the distribution of the entry (typically a family) and display the likely distribution of that family in the region, not that of the single representative species shown for that family. In the case of a genus or species entry, the map shown represents the distribution of that genus or species. Occasionally, the reader may find an insect outside of the shown distribution range

given in the map. This is because the maps give only the *probable distribution* range of the entry – detailed distributional data for most South African insects is not available. To complicate matters, insects are mobile and can change their distribution very rapidly in response to short-term climatic fluctuations.

❸ **Body size** is given in millimetres and defined either as body length or wingspan depending on the convention used for each group. In the case of family entries, component species may vary widely in size and a range is given.

# SPRINGTAILS
**Order Collembola**

Tiny, primitive, soft-bodied, wingless invertebrates. No longer considered true insects, but still conventionally included in insect guides. Best recognized by their unique ventral jumping organ ('furca') that folds under the abdomen. Globular or elongate, usually white or grey, mostly 1–3mm long. Among the most common and widespread of all animal groups, attaining abundances of 100,000 or more per m² in soil, leaf litter and other moist, sheltered habitats. Juveniles and adults similar in structure.

### Pudgy springtails
Family Neanuridae

**1–3mm** Fat, short-limbed, some with dorsal projections on the body. The slate-grey marine springtail *Anurida maritima* shown (length 3mm) is covered with tiny, water-repellent hairs. **BIOLOGY:** This species scavenges on dead or dying animals on rocky shores. **HABITAT:** Floats in rock pools at low tide, sheltering in crevices or among barnacle or mussel shells at high tide.

# DIPLURANS
**Order Diplura**

Technically not insects, but easily confused with silverfish and bristletails, so are conventionally included in insect guides. Pale, soft-bodied, eyeless and wingless, with elongate antennae made up of distinct, bead-like segments. Abdomen with 10 segments, ending in a pair of cerci – either long, slender and segmented or stout and pincer-like. Most of the 50 regional species are small (up to 5mm) and unpigmented, but a few grow up to 20mm and have darkened cerci. Found mostly under stones and in leaf litter in moist habitats. Females lay eggs in the soil; juveniles resemble small adults.

### Japygid diplurans
Family Japygidae

**10–20mm** 19 spp. in SA; unusually large and robust diplurans; abdomen elongate, widening and becoming darker posteriorly, terminal cerci modified into characteristic pincer-like structures, resembling an earwig's forceps. *Japyx* sp. shown. **BIOLOGY:** Predatory, using mouthparts and pincer-like cerci to capture prey. **HABITAT:** Under rotting logs, stones or leaf litter in moist habitats, like the forest floor.

# SILVERFISH
**Order Thysanura**

Primitive, wingless insects. Body soft, tapering, covered with tiny, overlapping scales with a metallic appearance and a greasy feel. Named for their colour and fish-like body movements. Abdomen ends in 3 equal, elongate, segmented caudal filaments. Mostly nocturnal. Use their long antennae and caudal filaments to feel their way; eyes small or absent. Introduced domestic forms very familiar, found among household books and papers. Indigenous species occur in forest litter or with ants or termites. Juveniles resemble small adults.

## Silverfish
Family Lepismatidae

**4–15mm** ± 40 spp. in SA; eyes small, body with small, silvery scales, abdomen tapers to 3 elongate 'tails'. Domestic silverfish *Ctenolepisma longicaudata* (shown), introduced from Europe, is very familiar. **BIOLOGY:** This species is nocturnal, cryptic, feeds on paper and fabrics and may damage books. Hides in cupboards, drawers and bookshelves; is often trapped in baths, sinks or bowls. May live 4 years and moults continuously. **HABITAT:** Abundant in buildings.

# BRISTLETAILS
**Order Archaeognatha**

Ancient wingless insects. Body elongate, tapers and ends in 3 filaments. Like silverfish, but with large compound eyes that meet on top of the head; thorax dorsally arched; central caudal filament much longer than lateral filaments. Jump by snapping the abdomen and caudal filaments downward. Confined to damp habitats, like leaf litter and moist soil under logs or rocks. Feed on mosses, lichens, algae and decaying organic matter. Young resemble adults. Lifespan unusually long, typically 3–4 years.

## Rock bristletails
Family Meinertellidae

**10–15 mm** ± 19 spp in SA; body mottled, with smooth, overlapping scales. Antennae elongate. Caudal appendages very long, held folded together directly behind the abdomen. Thorax strongly arched. *Machiloides* (shown) the most common genus in the region. **BIOLOGY:** Family mainly nocturnal, but active by day in moist habitats. **HABITAT:** Leaf litter, under bark or in dead wood, particularly in indigenous forests.

# MAYFLIES

**Order Ephemeroptera**

Adults delicate, eyes large, those of males sometimes divided into sections. Legs slender, the first pair in males sometimes enlarged to grip females in flight. Wings transparent and held folded above the body at rest, second pair often reduced or absent. Abdomen ends in 2–3 long caudal filaments. Lack functional mouthparts; adults do not feed, living a few hours or days and swarming over water to mate and lay eggs. Nymphs long-lived and more likely to be encountered, aquatic and make up a large proportion of fauna in mountain streams; an important food resource for fish. Their abdomens bear lateral gills and 3 (rarely 2) elongate tails.

## Small minnow mayflies
Family Baetidae
**nymphs 3–9mm, adults 4–14mm**
Most diverse and abundant mayfly family in SA, with ± 48 spp. Nymphs elongate, cylindrical, with 6–7 paired abdominal gills, each a single or double leaf-like plate (*Baetis* sp. shown). Adults (bottom pic) yellow to brown; forewings glassy, hindwings reduced to absent; 2 caudal filaments. Eyes of males in 2 sections, the upper part orange to red and raised on a stalk. **BIOLOGY:** Nymphs swim with minnow-like movement. **HABITAT:** Rapid streams; also still waters.

## Flathead mayflies
Family Heptageniidae
**nymphs 8–13mm, adults 7–12mm**
2 genera in SA; nymphs with broad, flattened, semicircular head, flat, tapering body and strong, sprawling legs (*Afronurus harrisoni* shown, length 8–12mm). Gills 1–6 flattened, leaf-like plates, each with a tuft of filaments at its base, gill 7 without filaments. Adults relatively large, yellow to brown, with 2 pairs of wings. Eyes of males huge, but not divided. **BIOLOGY:** Adults mostly nocturnal. **HABITAT:** Nymphs cling to rocks in fast-flowing waters.

## Prong-gilled mayflies
Family Leptophlebiidae
**nymphs 9–20mm, adults 8–12mm**
20 spp. in SA; nymphs slightly flattened, gill 1 absent or reduced, gills 2–7 double, spear-shaped or ending in multiple projections; have 3 long, equal caudal filaments (*Castanophlebia calida* shown, length 11mm). Adults with 2 pairs of wings; male's eyes with large upper and smaller lower sections. **BIOLOGY:** Nymphs feed by shredding leaf material. **HABITAT:** Usually in flowing waters.

## Squaregills (caenids) — Family Caenidae

**nymphs 3–10mm, adults 2–5mm**
6 spp. in SA; nymphs with first pair of gills filamentous, second pair enlarged into flattened, rectangular flaps covering the remaining pairs, which are frilly plates (*Caenis* sp. shown). Adults small, forewings with simple venation, often fringed with setae (hairs), hindwings absent, abdomen with 3 caudal filaments. **BIOLOGY:** Nymphs feed on detritus. **HABITAT:** Pools or silty backwaters.

## Pale burrowers — Family Polymitarcyidae

**nymphs 16mm, adults up to 20mm**
2 spp. in SA; nymphs large, with 'tusks' on the head and large, feathery gills folded over the back (*Povilla adusta* shown). Adults with weak or vestigial legs (except for male's forelegs). **BIOLOGY:** Filter-feed by pumping water through burrow with their gills. Adults live a few hours and perform mass-mating flights; dying females expel eggs on water surface. **HABITAT:** Nymphs burrow into river banks in slow waters.

## Water specs — Family Prosopistomatidae

**nymphs 3–4mm, adults up to 5mm** 1 genus in SA; nymphs tiny, oval; enlarged carapace covers thorax, gills and most of abdomen (*Prosopistoma* sp. shown). Caudal filaments very short. Adults very small, with no cross veins on wings. Females with atrophied legs. **BIOLOGY:** Emerge to mate at dawn, then die; females float on water and release eggs. **HABITAT:** Nymphs under stones in strong currents.

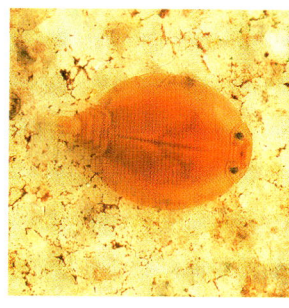

## Stout crawlers — Family Tricorythidae

**length 5–9mm** 1 genus described in SA; nymphs dark brown, slow-moving clamberers; use brush of setae projecting from mouthparts to collect detritus (*Tricorythus* sp. shown). Adults small, often dark; hindwings absent, venation of forewings simple; legs all similar in length. **BIOLOGY:** Emerge from stream at dusk and live for a few hours. **HABITAT:** Nymphs on undersides of stones in fast water.

**MAYFLIES**

## DAMSELFLIES AND DRAGONFLIES
**Order Odonata**

Adults have 2 pairs of heavily veined, clear wings. Damselflies (**Demoiselles to Featherlegs**) are small, delicate, with narrow, equal-sized fore- and hindwings. Dragonflies (**Clubtails to Wandering glider**) are larger; hindwings broader. Both have a wing spot ('pterostigma') at the leading margin of each wing. Antennae short, bristle-like; abdomen long, thin, ending in claspers in males. Mating pairs form 'mating wheel'. Frequent water bodies. Nymphs aquatic, predaceous with enlarged, toothed lower lip ('labial mask') that is shot out to seize prey. Damselfly nymphs slender with external gills, dragonfly nymphs stouter, breathing via rectal gills.

### Demoiselles
Family Calopterygidae

**wingspan 80mm** Glistening demoiselle *Phaon irridipennis* is the only Calopterygid in the region. Body large, light brown, metallic green to bronze dorsally, wings unstalked, legs very long. Nymph's labial mask very long, grooved at the end. **BIOLOGY:** Perches on riverine plants and engages in fluttering courtship. **HABITAT:** Forested streams and larger bushveld rivers in warmer parts of the region.

### Jewels
Family Chlorocyphidae

**wingspan 45–50mm** 3 spp. in SA; medium-sized; abdomen broad, bright blue or red. Dancing jewel *Platycypha caligata* (shown, wingspan 45mm) with abdomen sky blue, thorax red and flattened and tibiae broad, with red outer and white inner surfaces. Nymphs with a very small notch at end of the labial mask. **BIOLOGY:** In courtship dance, male *P. caligata* sways in flight, flashes his red outer tibiae and vibrates his legs to show off the white inner surfaces. **HABITAT:** Rocky forest streams.

### Spreadwings
Family Lestidae

**wingspan 40–75mm** 7 spp. in SA (*Lestes* sp. shown); small to large; body green, yellow-brown or black. Each wing with very long pterostigma. Nymph's labial mask very thin, expanding rapidly near the end, terminal teeth covered with hairs. **BIOLOGY:** At rest, Lestidae hold the wings partially open, and the abdomen hangs downward. Life cycle is rapid, adapted to erratic rainfall. **HABITAT:** Widespread in sluggish streams and pans; adults often occur far from water.

## Malachites
Family Synlestidae (Chlorolestidae)

**wingspan 50–85mm** 8 spp. endemic to SA, with 2 genera, *Chlorolestes* and *Ecclorolestes*. Large; body metallic green, some males with chalk-white wing bands. Nymph's labial mask with short terminal cleft, teeth lack hairs. *C. umbratus* (adult shown, wingspan 50mm) has nymph with dark stripe through each paddle-like gill. **BIOLOGY:** Synlestidae lay eggs in young shoots of plants above water level; hatched nymphs fall into the water. **HABITAT:** Mountain streams.

## Threadtails
Family Protoneuridae

**wingspan 35–60mm** 2 spp. in SA; medium-sized; body black or blue. Male Grey threadtail *Ellatoneura glauca* (shown, wingspan 40mm) has pale blue thorax with thin, horizontal black stripe; abdomen black dorsally, white ventrally. Females and immatures pale tan. **BIOLOGY:** *E. glauca* occurs in groups. **HABITAT:** Locally abundant along shaded stream banks.

## Pond damsels
Family Coenagrionidae

**wingspan 20–65mm** ± 41 spp. in SA. Mostly small; encountered at pans, vleis, marshes and slow-flowing rivers. Colour variable. Identified by combination of short pterostigma, male's claspers short (not forming forceps) and wings held together over thorax at rest. May be confused with threadtails (Protoneuridae) and featherlegs (Platycnemidae). Nymphs with characteristic cone-shaped bulge between the jaws.

## Common pond damsel
*Ceriagron glabrum*

**wingspan 46mm** Medium-sized; thorax pale orange, abdomen red or orange in male, olive-brown in female. Thoracic stripes absent in both sexes. **BIOLOGY:** Makes short foray flights from perches. **HABITAT:** Common in water bodies fringed with dense reed beds. Reaches Madagascar, the Indian Ocean islands and even Australia.

### March bluetail *Ischnura senegalensis*

**wingspan 38mm** Small; male blue with underside of abdomen tan and wing spot divided into blue-and-white triangles (cf. Swamp bluet, *Africallagma glaucum*, below). Female with pale green or orange thorax. **BIOLOGY:** Adults fly October–June. **HABITAT:** Ubiquitous in slow-flowing rivers, vleis, dams and even saline water. Reaches Central Africa and India.

### Swamp bluet *Africallagma glaucum*

**wingspan 34mm** Small; mature male sky blue, blue-green or black with abdomen blue below (cf. March bluetail, *Ischnura senegalensis*, above). Female greenish or yellowish. Nymph slender, pale green with 3 large, flattened, translucent gills at end of the abdomen. **BIOLOGY:** Flies close to water, perching on low vegetation. **HABITAT:** Very common at water bodies, including brackish pans. Reaches Central Africa.

### Featherlegs Family Platycnemidae

**wingspan 65mm** 4 spp. in SA; medium-sized; body brown, wings amber. Male and female Gold-tail dragonflies *Allocnemis leucosticta* (shown, wingspan 50mm) have brown wings, with striking white pterostigma on all wings and thorax striped pale blue. Nymphs squat, with spindly, banded legs and thick, sausage-like gills. **BIOLOGY:** *A. leucosticta* often found in groups on twigs. **HABITAT:** Rocky mountain streams.

### Clubtails Family Gomphidae

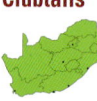

**wingspan 50–95mm** 15 spp. in SA; medium-sized or large; the only dragonflies with widely separated eyes. Green and black or yellow and black, with striped abdomen. Common tigertail *Ictinogomphus ferox* (shown, wingspan 90mm) has yellow-and-black striped abdomen; male has prominent yellow claspers at end of abdomen. **BIOLOGY:** Clubtails make short foray flights from mud or stones. **HABITAT:** Common along vegetated or rocky streams and ponds.

# Hawkers

Family Aeschnidae

**wingspan 80–140mm** 11 spp. in SA; includes the largest of dragonflies. Huge, brightly coloured eyes meet in the middle of the head. They patrol large territories and feed on a range of insects, including other dragonflies.

## Friendly hawker *Zosteraeschna minuscula*

**wingspan 80mm** Large, body with yellow-and-brown stripes, base of hindwings with small incision at the base, head with T-shaped black marking in front of the eyes. Female and immature with amber tint to wings. **BIOLOGY:** Flies low over water, settling frequently, easily approached. **HABITAT:** Still waters in ponds and vleis, less common at mountain streams. Also occurs in Namibia.

## Blue emperor *Anax imperator*

**wingspan 105mm** Very large; abdomen turquoise and thorax green in both sexes. Young nymphs strikingly banded in cream and black, larger ones green, attaining 55mm. **BIOLOGY:** Female uses serrated ovipositor to pierce plant tissue for egg laying. Adults migratory, occurring spring–autumn and often preying on large dragonflies such as the Wandering glider *Pantala flavescens* (p.20). Nymphs eat tadpoles and fish. **HABITAT:** Mainly slow-flowing rivers, vleis and dams.

# Skimmers

Family Libellulidae

**wingspan 34–90mm** ± 58 spp. in SA; the most commonly encountered dragonflies, typically blue or red, although coloration develops fully only in mature males. They undertake brief forays from perches to which they often return. Nymphs have a convex, cupped mouthpart used to capture prey.

## Red-veined dropwing *Trithemis arteriosa*

**wingspan 54mm** Medium-sized, with black marks at the end of the thin abdomen. Male has red body with red veins in the front margin of the wings; female and immature dull yellow. Nymph oval, hairless, with spines on top of the body. **BIOLOGY:** Male defends territory from a perch near the water surface. **HABITAT:** Widespread across the region, as well as throughout the rest of Africa and the Mediterranean; occurs near most types of water body.

### Little scarlet — *Crocothemis sanguinolenta*

**wingspan 52mm** Medium-sized red dragonfly, recognizable by its broad abdomen, red pterostigma and amber patches at the base of the wings. Female is yellowish. **BIOLOGY:** Common in summer. **HABITAT:** A cosmopolitan species found on rocks and twigs along the reeded margins of ponds and streams.

### Dark dropwing (Navy dropwing)
*Trithemis furva*

**wingspan 59mm** Medium-sized; male uniform cobalt blue, female and immature yellow with black markings. May be confused with other similar blue *Trithemis* spp. **BIOLOGY:** Common in late summer; flight slow and agile. **HABITAT:** Widespread at most kinds of water bodies across the region up to equatorial Africa.

### Yellow-veined widow — *Palpopleura jucunda*

**wingspan 35mm** Very small, with considerable size variation; stout yellow-and-black striped body, wings clear with orange tint and yellow veins over black markings. **BIOLOGY:** Flight brief, settles frequently on vegetation. **HABITAT:** Occurs at small, well-vegetated pools, vleis and rivers, but most common in swamps and marshes. Extends to Central Africa.

### Wandering glider — *Pantala flavescens*

**wingspan 80mm** Body orange-yellow; wings clear, sometimes with faint yellow tinge at bases and tips. Nymph hairless and large with strong spines at end of the abdomen. **BIOLOGY:** Migrates ahead of storms with gliding flight and lays eggs in temporary pools; voracious larvae develop very rapidly. **HABITAT:** Found in most habitats, often far from water; a common species in the warmer parts of the world.

**DAMSELFLIES AND DRAGONFLIES**

# COCKROACHES
**Order Blattodea**

Head is almost covered by a large shield (the 'pronotal shield' or 'pronotum'); the running legs have a large segment at the base (the 'coxa'). Forewings ('tegmina') are leathery, hindwings are membranous with large, folded, fan-like area on inner margin. Females often wingless. Most species are nocturnal. Abdomen ends in a pair of short segments, known as 'cerci'; in some it may have scent glands. Females produce a leathery egg case ('ootheca'), often carried about while attached to the end of the abdomen. A few species are associated with human habitation, where they are pests, but most are restricted to undisturbed habitats, such as leaf litter, caves, dense vegetation and spaces under bark and stones. Many endemic genera and species occur in SA, especially in the southwestern Cape.

## Common cockroaches
**Family Blattidae**

**length 14–37mm** ± 50 spp. in SA; medium-sized to large cockroaches, forelegs with many spines on the front of the femur (the thickest leg segment). Ootheca always carried at the end of the abdomen.

### American cockroach  *Periplaneta americana*

**length 27–34mm** Large reddish-brown cockroach; one of the commonest pest species in human habitation worldwide. **BIOLOGY:** Both sexes winged and capable of fluttering flight. Uses scent glands to attract others, which form swarms. Ootheca carried for only a brief period, and then dropped. **HABITAT:** Aggregates in warm areas, behind fridges and stoves for instance. Probably originated in tropical Africa.

### Red-headed cockroach
*Deropeltis erythrocephala*

**length 27–37mm** Male has long black wings; female is wingless. Legs and head orange-red. All species of *Deropeltis* have a large pad on the hindtarsi. **BIOLOGY:** Occurs in groups of slow-moving adults and nymphs. Does not produce aggregation odour. **HABITAT:** Found under flat stones that rest on rocks, or in tree stumps. Occasionally enters houses.

### Leaproach
*Saltoblattella montistabularis*

**length 8mm** The only known jumping cockroach; was first described in 2010. Body is adapted for leaping and resembles that of a small grasshopper. Wings reduced to small pads, hindlegs huge and grasshopper-like. Eyes bulging and body narrow in male. **BIOLOGY:** An active, diurnal cockroach, moves mostly by jumping between grass stems. **HABITAT:** Frequents low fynbos vegetation.

### Blattellid cockroaches
Family Blattellidae

**length 5–20mm** Very diverse family with 75 spp. in SA; small, lightly built, agile cockroaches. Females carry ootheca until just before the eggs hatch, but rotate the case so that its keel faces downward. Males have glands on the abdomen that produce a secretion on which females feed just prior to mating.

### German cockroach
*Blattella germanica*

**length 11mm** Amber brown with 2 dark stripes running along length of the pronotum. Both sexes winged. **BIOLOGY:** Flies well. Secretes an aggregation pheromone that stimulates clustering of family groups; male also secretes pheromones to attract female. **HABITAT:** A domestic pest species introduced from Asia, but now cosmopolitan. Often seeks warmth behind electrical equipment.

### Cape zebra cockroach
*Temnopteryx phalerata*

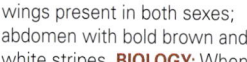
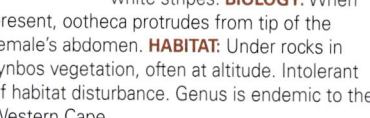

**length 20mm** Flattened; short wings present in both sexes; abdomen with bold brown and white stripes. **BIOLOGY:** When present, ootheca protrudes from tip of the female's abdomen. **HABITAT:** Under rocks in fynbos vegetation, often at altitude. Intolerant of habitat disturbance. Genus is endemic to the Western Cape.

## Blaberid cockroaches
*Family Blaberidae*

**length 7–50mm** Diverse family of medium-sized to large cockroaches with approximately 90 spp. in SA; sluggish and heavily built. Ootheca retained within the body, often resulting in young being born alive. Spines absent from undersides of the mid- and hindtibiae.

### Table Mountain cockroach *Aptera fusca*

**length 30–40mm** Female large, bulky and wingless, male slimmer and winged. Body rich reddish brown, with yellow margins. **BIOLOGY:** Female cares for young and adopts tail-up position when disturbed, emitting a squeaking sound (as air is forced through her breathing tubes). Sunbathes in the early morning on top of bushes. **HABITAT:** Low fynbos vegetation, often in exposed positions.

### Bark cockroaches *Derocalymma* spp.

**length 20mm** Medium-sized, with oval, dark brown body, pronotum triangular with ridges along each side. Male with fairly long, rough-textured wings. Female wingless. **BIOLOGY:** Body covered with sensory granules. Individuals never form groups. **HABITAT:** Common under the loose bark of dead and living trees, especially in open woodland. Flies readily to lights.

## Pseudophyllodromid cockroaches
*Family Pseudophyllodromiidae*

**length 14–22mm** Small, diverse and resembling Blattellidae (p.22). Legs, antennae and wings long. Ootheca either deposited on the ground or carried inside the body, but never rotated as in Blattellidae, so keel always faces upward.

### Banded cockroach *Supella dimidiata*

**length 17 mm** Body narrow, wings long in male and marked with black spots; female with very short wings. Nymph with black pronotum. **BIOLOGY:** Very fast and agile. Male attracted to lights. Female releases secretion from the abdomen to attract males. **HABITAT:** Widespread over a range of habitats, often in tree foliage and under bark. The related Brown-banded cockroach *S. longipalpa* is a pest of homes in North America and the United Kingdom.

# TERMITES

Order Isoptera

Relatively small order (about 200 spp. in the region) of abundant, economically important, plant-feeding, social insects. They construct conspicuous earth mounds above the soil, or live in galleries in dry wood. All are truly social, having castes of reproductive individuals, sterile workers and soldiers. Soldiers have a range of defensive head structures, including powerful jaws and nozzle-like, jawless heads that can eject chemical sprays. Now considered to be closely related to cockroaches (order Blattodea, p.21) and commonly included with them, and with the mantids (p.26), in the super-order Dictyoptera.

## Harvester termites

Family Hodotermitidae

**length 7–15mm** 2 spp. in SA; large, common and conspicuous termites with pigmented workers; all castes have compound eyes and mandibles with many inner teeth. They nest wholly or partially below ground, and workers are commonly seen foraging en masse, mostly in the late afternoon during summer, but during the day in winter.

### Northern harvester termite
*Hodotermes mossambicus*

**length 8–15mm** Workers with dark brown head capsule and brown-and-cream striped abdomen. Soldiers, seen less often, have a larger, red-brown head and robust, curved black jaws. **BIOLOGY:** Workers emerge from underground nests to feed on both live and dead grass. Cut grass is stored in chambers around the spherical subterranean nests, which house the reproductives. **HABITAT:** Found in most vegetation types in the summer-rainfall parts of the region.

### Southern harvester termite
*Microhodotermes viator*

**length 7–13mm** Workers have a dark brown head and reddish-brown body with darker brown stripes; soldiers with reddish head and curved black jaws (queen in centre). **BIOLOGY:** Ubiquitous in the winter-rainfall regions of South Africa, where workers forage from mounds that may be either 1–2m-tall, domed clay nests, or *heuweltjies*, that is, domed nests covered with a thick sand layer. Faecal (frass) outpourings accumulate on both nest types. **HABITAT:** Occurs in renosterveld, succulent karoo and Nama-karoo vegetation types.

## Subterranean termites  Family Rhinotermitidae

**length 5–8mm** 7 spp. in SA (some alien), the commonest being the Sand termite *Psammotermes allocerus*. Family members have a frontal gland that opens from a short, conical projection on the head. **BIOLOGY:** Nests are small (35cm in diameter), inconspicuous, and situated at the base of grass clumps. In Namibia, Rhinotermitidae are closely associated with fairy circles (unvegetated, evenly spaced circles in grassland areas). **HABITAT:** Restricted to the arid, sandy parts of the region. May damage fence posts and timber trusses in roofs.

## Higher termites
Family Termitidae

**length 4–20mm** Most of the world's termite species belong to this large family, which includes 190 regional species. Nests range from massive clay towers to small, inconspicuous structures; some species live within the nests of other termite species. The pronotum is saddle-shaped with lobes that hang down the sides.

## Large fungus-growing termite
*Macrotermes natalensis*

**length 5–18mm, soldiers largest** Both small and large soldiers have a massive orange head capsule, with slender, untoothed jaws that cross over when closed. Very large, domed clay nests may exceed 2m in height and may have numerous pinnacles, each with a wide chimney. **BIOLOGY:** Cultivates fungi grown on macerated plant matter. **HABITAT:** The commonest species in the genus, its mounds are sometimes abundant in dry, open veld and bushveld.

## Common fungus-growing termite
*Odontotermes badius*

**length 9mm** Workers pale; larger soldiers (centre) all similar in size, with single tooth on inner margins of jaws. Winged reproductives ('flying ants') have dark heads and wings. Nests largely subterranean, with subtle, vegetation-covered mounds covered with excavated soil dumps. **BIOLOGY:** Forages under cover of cemented sand on all forms of dry vegetable matter, including dung and wood. May be very destructive in homes. **HABITAT:** Most veld types; also in buildings.

### Snouted harvester termites
*Trinervitermes* spp.

**length 5mm** Soldiers have head modified into a snout, with reduced mandibles; large and smaller soldiers are present. Nests are domed clay structures 0.5–1m in height. **BIOLOGY:** Harvest grass at night via tunnels radiating from nest. Soldiers eject sticky threads of terpene-containing glue to repel enemies. **HABITAT:** Most common termite in moist veld.

### Black-mound termite
*Amitermes hastatus*

**length 4mm** Soldiers have curved mandibles with a single, internal tooth halfway down each. Abdomen swollen and packed with grey material. Nests dark grey-black, up to 35cm tall. Colonies slow-growing. Soldiers produce a defensive chemical from head gland. **BIOLOGY:** Feeds on decaying and dead wood. Faecal pellets used to construct nest mound. **HABITAT:** Common in fynbos and many other vegetation types.

## MANTIDS
Order Mantodea

Smallish order (<200 spp. in SA); relatively large, predaceous insects related to termites and cockroaches. All have an elongated first thoracic segment ('prothorax') and spiny, well-developed, raptorial ('grasping') forelimbs – adaptations for lunging at prey. Eggs are laid in a foamy egg case ('ootheca'), which then hardens. Nymphs wingless, adults usually winged: narrow, slightly hardened forewings ('tegmina') protect the large fan-like hindwings. Small, tail-like 'cerci' project from end of the abdomen.

### Flower mantids
Family Hymenopodidae

**length 30–50mm** Masters of camouflage, mimicking flowers or dead leaves. Head with a prong-like projection, legs with flattened lobes, forewings may have eyespots. Enlarged front femora have alternating groups of short and long spines.

### Leaf mantid
*Phyllocrania paradoxica*

**length 44mm** Leaf-like projection on the head; male with dark cross at the base of the folded wings, female light brown with more extensive flanges on prothorax and abdomen than male. Legs with extensive flanges, larger in females. Ootheca long and slender with thin prong at one end. **BIOLOGY:** Swaying movements perfect the camouflage. **HABITAT:** In shrubs and bushes in subtropical region.

### Eye-flower mantid  *Pseudocreobotra wahlbergii*

**length 42mm** Legs banded in green and yellow, forewings yellow, each with a convincing eyespot on a green patch. Nymph mottled green, pink and pale yellow, bearing an eyespot on top of the abdomen. **BIOLOGY:** Preys on large pollinators, including bees and wasps, which are subdued with the formidable spiny forelegs. **HABITAT:** Occurs in subtropical grassland and forest; usually perched on flowers.

### Flower mantid  *Harpagomantis tricolor*

**length 31mm** Smaller and duller version of Eye-flower mantid, *P. wahlbergii* (above), with green-and-yellow bands on the tegmina. Two forward-projecting spines on front of the face. Top part of eyes pointed. **BIOLOGY:** A common mantid, sitting in exposed positions, often on flower heads. **HABITAT:** Low vegetation in most habitats, especially grassland.

### Common mantids                                         Family Mantidae

**length 11–80mm** The largest family of mantids, with ± 140 spp. in SA; includes most of the familiar, commonly encountered green or brown mantids. They have alternating rows of short and long spines on the enlarged foretibiae. Abundant in most vegetation types across the region; some are useful predators that consume harmful insects in gardens.

### Common green mantid  *Sphodromantis gastrica*

**length 55mm** Heavily built, especially the female, which is usually short-winged and flightless. Body apple green, top of abdomen white and yellow. Nymph curls abdomen above body. Ootheca a familiar light brown foam structure cemented to walls or tree trunks. (Bottom image shows female depositing the ootheca.) **BIOLOGY:** Feeds largely on caterpillars. **HABITAT:** Common in most vegetation types; also in gardens and among crops.

MANTIDS

### Bark mantids
*Tarachodes* spp.

**length 37mm** Excellent bark mimics, usually grey in colour. Many have brushes of hairs on the limbs, which are flattened against the substrate when at rest, reducing shadows and perfecting the mimicry. Females typically wingless. **BIOLOGY:** Fast-moving predators of caterpillars on tree trunks. Females guard ootheca for 2 months until nymphs hatch. **HABITAT:** Tree trunks in warm, summer-rainfall woodland.

### Marbled mantid
*Polyspilota aeruginosa*

**length 80mm** Very large green-and-brown mantid; insides of foretibiae blue, with a distinctive black spot. Wings mottled brown. **BIOLOGY:** An aggressive predator that displays the warning coloration on the inner part of its forelegs when threatened. **HABITAT:** Trees and tall grass in subtropical summer-rainfall regions; widespread across Africa and Madagascar.

### Grass mantid
*Pyrgomantis rhodesica*

**length 70mm** Grass-stalk mimic, with elongated and cylindrical brown body; eyes long, oval and matching contour of the head; forelegs small, with pink on the inner margin. Head extended into a long cone to complete the mimicry. **BIOLOGY:** Often short-winged and incapable of flight. **HABITAT:** Grassland in summer-rainfall regions.

### Ground mantids
*Ligariella* spp.

**length 11mm** Genus of mantids with shortened bodies, cryptically coloured in pink and orange to match the quartz pebbles among which they forage. Head large, legs slender and striped, wings absent. **BIOLOGY:** Ground-dwelling mantids that run rapidly. **HABITAT:** Bare patches of stony ground, typically in arid parts.

## Stick mantid
*Popa undata*

**length 55mm** Heavily built, large grey mantids that superficially resemble bark mantids (p.28), but are largely terrestrial and rarely occur on trees. The top of each body segment and the legs are ornamented with protruding knobs and small spikes. **BIOLOGY:** Fast-running; typically incapable of flight. **HABITAT:** Dry parts of the region, often in grassland or woodland.

## Large grass mantid
*Hoplocoryphella grandis*

**length 60mm** Large and slender, body light brown, with small but wide head and quite delicate raptorial forelegs. Hindwings smoky brown, with light spot at wing tips. Ootheca a remarkable, partially hollow, oval bubble (bottom image). **BIOLOGY:** Female short-winged ('brachypterous') and incapable of flight; male attracted to lights. **HABITAT:** Arid open woodland.

## Gargoyle mantids
Family Empusidae

**length 70–85mm** Very large and striking mantids with a sharp prong on top of the head; antennae comb-like in males but thread-like in females. Long, spindly legs adorned with flattened flanges. Body pale yellow and pink, wings green, shading to orange at the wing tips. *Empusa guttula* (shown, length 74mm) is the most common species; its prothorax is expanded at the origin of the forelegs. The nymphs (bottom image) have very slender bodies; all body parts have remarkable foliage-like projections; this provides them with excellent camouflage. **BIOLOGY:** Formidable predators. **HABITAT:** A variety of vegetation types across the country, usually in shrubs.

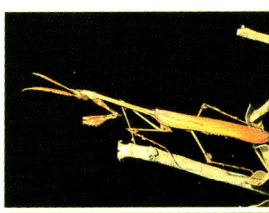

# EARWIGS
**Order Dermaptera**

Medium-sized brown-black insects with oval, fan-like hindwings, which are folded carefully after flight under the very small and square protective forewings ('tegmina'), using a pair of large, hardened forceps (modified cerci) at the end of the telescopic abdomen. Usually found in litter or crevices in vegetation. Diet ranges from plant matter to small insects. Females tend eggs that are laid in burrows. Nymphs, and the females of some species, are wingless.

## Long-horned earwigs
Family Labiduridae

**length 20–30mm** 16 spp. in SA; appearance differs widely between species, but family members recognizable by the round second segment of the 'foot' (tarsus), which does not extend beneath the third segment. Antennae long, with 16–30 segments.

### Striped earwig
*Labidura riparia*

**length 30mm** Large, pale earwig with a stripe extending along the narrow tegmina, orange head and prothorax and a dark marking along the centre of the abdomen. Forceps very large and strong in the male. **BIOLOGY:** When threatened, holds forceps over the body; also uses them to capture small insects. **HABITAT:** Cosmopolitan; typically found under rocks and debris along beaches and river banks.

### Ring-legged earwig
*Euboriella annulipes*

**length 20mm** No vestige of wings; legs banded in pale orange and brown, forceps small, stout and asymmetrical. Antennae with <20 segments. **BIOLOGY:** A nocturnal detritus-feeder. **HABITAT:** Cosmopolitan, often found in disturbed habitats such as compost heaps in gardens.

### Common earwigs
Family Forficulidae

**length 8mm** 8 spp. in SA; recognized by the second tarsal segment extending around to partially cover the third segment. Antennae with 10–15 segments. *Forficula senegalensis* (shown, length 8mm) is widespread in coastal parts of the region and has contrasting black abdomen and orange body and legs. Forceps highly variable in size. **BIOLOGY:** Common earwigs feed mainly on plant matter and reportedly capture small insects. **HABITAT:** A range of moist habitats.

# STONEFLIES
### Order Plecoptera

Small order of stream insects. Adults always occur in the vicinity of water bodies, generally rivers or streams. They fly very weakly and have 2 pairs of wings, which are held over the body at rest, and a short to long pair of cerci at the end of the abdomen. Nymphs are aquatic and may have fluffy gills at the base of each leg, although smaller nymphs in well-oxygenated mountain streams lack gills. Mature nymphs crawl out of the water onto shoreline logs or rocks to emerge from their nymphal skins (or 'shucks'), which remain attached to the place of emergence.

## True stoneflies
### Family Perlidae

**length 20–25mm** 1 genus, *Neoperla* (shown, length 25mm), with at least 6 similar-looking spp. in SA. Large, yellowish stoneflies; both adults and nymphs have long cerci at the end of the abdomen. Compound eyes large, wings folded flat over body. Nymphs dark brown with yellow markings and gills at the base of the legs. **BIOLOGY:** Adults attracted to lights. Nymphs voracious predators, feeding on blackfly larvae (p.91) and other aquatic insects. **HABITAT:** Both large, slow-flowing, turbid rivers and clear mountain streams in summer-rainfall region.

## Southern stoneflies
### Family Notonemouridae

**length 4–8mm** Among the smallest known stoneflies, with ± 40 spp. in SA. Adults common in mountain streams, particularly in the Western and Eastern Cape; they are lead grey and fold their wings into a tight tube around the body; cerci are single stumps. Nymphs have long cerci and generally resemble wingless adults. Their presence is indicative of good water quality.

## Porcupine stoneflies
*Desmonemoura* spp.

**length 5mm** Adults recognized by their brown-and-pale yellow striped wings and orange prothorax and legs. Nymphs have few body hairs, and, when nearing maturity, have banded wing pads. **BIOLOGY:** Adults unusual for southern stoneflies in emerging in early summer, not winter. **HABITAT:** Fast-flowing mountain streams with cobble beds.

### Cape stoneflies
*Aphanicerca* spp.

**length 5mm** Greyish brown, with characteristic clear patch at end of the forewings. Nymphs smooth, with a fringe of fine hairs along the inner margin of the antennae. **BIOLOGY:** One of the most commonly encountered genera of southern stoneflies; nymphs play an important role in shredding and decomposing plant matter in mountain streams. Males tap on the substrate to attract females. **HABITAT:** Restricted to mountain streams.

## CRICKETS, KATYDIDS, GRASSHOPPERS AND LOCUSTS
### Order Orthoptera

Medium-sized to large (length 5–100mm), with a bulky body and broad, blunt head. Hindlegs are enlarged and modified for jumping. Forewings narrow and leathery, protecting the broad membranous hindwings that are folded beneath them (wingless or short-winged species are also common). All have chewing mouthparts and most are herbivorous. Among the few invertebrates that communicate using sounds produced by stridulatory (file-like) organs on the hindlegs and detected by 'ears' on the forelegs. Females often have sword-like ovipositors used to deposit eggs in soil or plant tissue. Juveniles resemble small, wingless adults.

### King crickets (Parktown prawns)
Family Anostostomatidae

**length up to 70mm** 14 spp. in SA; large, brown to reddish. Mandibles greatly enlarged in males of many species, as are the palps (sensory organs on the mouthparts), which are used to fight with other males. Shelter in underground burrows by day, emerging by night to feed on small animals and plant matter. Produce sounds by rubbing their legs against the abdomen. Life cycle relatively long, eggs taking up to 18 months to hatch, and adults living 1–3 years.

### Barred king crickets
*Onosandrus* spp.

**length 28mm** ± 8 African spp. in the genus. Stocky; cream with black bars extending onto the hindfemora, which are thickened basally. Females have long ovipositors. Genus is recognized by the presence of a single spine inside the upper part of foretibia. Mandibles equal in size and unmodified in both sexes (cf. Parktown prawn, p.33). **BIOLOGY:** Roam around at night to feed. **HABITAT:** Wet soils; also under rotting logs.

### Parktown prawn (King cricket)
*Libanasidus vittatus*

**length 60–70mm** Heavily built; head and thorax reddish, abdomen with orange and black bands, legs orange. Male with tusk-like mandibles, female with curved ovipositor. **BIOLOGY:** Nocturnal, emerging from burrow to feed on plant and animal matter and droppings. When disturbed, buzzes and ejects foul-smelling faeces. **HABITAT:** Forest litter; now common in the suburbs of Johannesburg.

### Jerusalem crickets    Family Stenopelmatidae

**length 20–40mm** 4 spp. in SA; large, brown to black, always wingless. Males often with enlarged mandibles; can inflict a severe bite. *Sia pallidus* (shown) is cream with a black-banded abdomen and honey-coloured head, thorax and legs. **BIOLOGY:** Jerusalem crickets remain in burrows by day, emerging to feed on plant or animal matter by night. **HABITAT:** *S. pallidus* favours dry sandy soil, particularly in coastal dunes; burrows under stones.

### Leaf-rolling crickets    Family Gryllacrididae

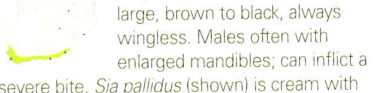

**length 15mm** ± 10 spp. in SA; predominantly tropical, robust, medium-sized, non-jumping crickets, with soft bodies and very long antennae. Adults of most species have fully formed wings, but some are wingless (as in *Emerus*, shown) or short-winged. All are mute. **BIOLOGY:** Use a silk-like oral secretion to bind tree leaves into a nest. Thought to be nocturnal carnivores of other insects and spiders. **HABITAT:** In folded leaves of trees and shrubs.

### Dune crickets    Family Schizodactylidae

**length 11mm** 7 spp. in SA; medium-sized, pale, with long petal-like extensions to tarsi for digging and to facilitate walking over loose sand. Most lack wings (as in *Comicus*, shown, length 11mm), but some can jump several metres. **BIOLOGY:** Emerge from burrows at night, resting in sandy depressions with outstretched antennae, waiting for insect prey. Males call by rubbing femora of the hindlegs against the abdomen. **HABITAT:** Sandy areas.

**CRICKETS AND THEIR RELATIVES**

### Camel crickets
Family Rhaphidophoridae

**length 10mm** 2 spp. in SA; wingless, humpbacked, with very long appendages and antennae; body covered with fine golden hairs. *Speleiacris tabulae* shown (length 10mm). **BIOLOGY:** Scavenge on decaying matter in caves, especially guano and dead bats. Run and jump well. **HABITAT:** Moist cave walls and rocks. *S. tabulae*, from caves and grottoes on the Cape Peninsula, requires high humidity to survive. *S. monslamiensis* found in Ceres mountains.

### Armoured ground crickets
Family Bradyporidae

**length 21–50mm** ± 30 endemic spp. in SA. Large, fat crickets lacking hindwings, rudimentary forewings hidden under hind edge of the large, spiny thoracic plate. Primarily herbivorous, but will scavenge and turn cannibalistic, devouring road-killed individuals. When threatened, they produce noxious secretions from pores on the thorax. Eaten by just a few animals, including bat-eared foxes, jackals and large birds. Eggs laid in small groups in soil. Restricted to arid and semiarid zones of southern Africa.

### Green corn cricket
*Acanthoplus armiventris*

**length 21mm** Fairly small species with red antennae, yellow pronotum with black spines, and brown, yellow and green abdomen. **BIOLOGY:** Rare in some years, but reaches outbreak proportions in others. Feeds chiefly on *Acacia* leaves. Male produces high-pitched vibrating call to attract females. Eggs laid in batches of 3–11 in the soil under trees. When alarmed, drops from vegetation, the male producing short alarm chirps. When handled, squirts yellow 'blood' (haemolymph) from the thorax. **HABITAT:** Found in low thorn trees, scrub and subtropical bushveld.

### Grey corn cricket
*Hetrodes pupus*

**length 36mm** Brown to grey, with small black spines on top of the abdomen; has 4 short spines on the pronotum in a square pattern. **BIOLOGY:** Heard more often than seen; male produces penetrating, buzzing courtship 'call' with his small forewings. Female lays a few very large eggs in a pod; eggs capable of drought dormancy. **HABITAT:** Various vegetation types, including strandveld, fynbos and succulent vegetation; most common within 60km of the shoreline.

**CRICKETS AND THEIR RELATIVES**

# Katydids and bush crickets
Family Tettigoniidae

**length 10–110mm** Diverse family with ± 160 spp. in SA. Large, 'long-horned' grasshoppers, including many vegetation mimics. Have long, thin antennae, 4-segmented tarsi and a pair of small 'ears' on the tibiae of the forelegs. Nocturnal and typically live in dense vegetation; some arid-adapted species in caves, overhangs and rock cracks. Males produce complex courtship calls using their modified forewings. Females use conspicuous, sword-like egg-laying tube ('ovipositor') at end of the abdomen to insert eggs into plant tissue or crevices. Although most feed on plant parts, some larger species are carnivorous.

## Oblong-eyed leaf katydids
*Eurycorypha* spp.

**length 21mm** At least 10 spp. in SA; large and bulky leaf mimics, all with elongated, oval eyes. Tegmina with distinct bend, lending a humpbacked profile. A thin yellow line typically runs along the tegmina, prothorax and eyes. **BIOLOGY:** Females use their ovipositors to make slits in leaves, into which eggs are laid. After a few months these hatch into dark, ant-like nymphs that mingle with ants for protection. **HABITAT:** Always associated with trees.

## Winged predatory katydid
*Clonia wahlbergi*

**length 40–65mm** 27 related spp. from SA. Very large; tegmina long and thin, hindwings fan-like and banded. Body green with silvery patches. All legs bear strong white spines. **BIOLOGY:** Voracious nocturnal predator of other large insects. Powerful jaws can bite severely. Male produces a low, buzzing call. Eggs laid in the ground at the bases of bushes. **HABITAT:** Fairly widespread in the region, occurring in bushveld, on forest edges and in tall grassland.

## Large leaf katydid
*Zabalius aridus*

**length 60mm** Large leaf mimic with small orange tubercles on the pronotum, and blue-and-orange hindlegs that are displayed when disturbed. Nymph pale green, short-limbed, with thin yellow stripe running along centre of the body. **BIOLOGY:** Nocturnal, feeding on young shoots of trees, especially figs. Seen throughout the year, often attracted to lights. Male's call a series of very high-pitched chirps at short intervals. **HABITAT:** Wooded areas across a range of vegetation types, also in suburbs where fig trees occur.

**CRICKETS AND THEIR RELATIVES**

### Bark katydid
*Cymatomera denticollis*

**length 55mm** Large bark and lichen mimic, displaying abdomen with yellow, red and black stripes when grasped. Hindwings large with light brown bands. **BIOLOGY:** Usually seen when attracted to lights. When disturbed, raises wings and may release a foul-smelling volatile substance from the abdomen. **HABITAT:** Dry woodland in subtropical parts of the region.

### Crickets
Family Gryllidae

**length 5–40mm** At least 70 spp. in SA. Well known and more often heard than seen. Have a 3-segmented tarsus, long, thin antennae and a well-developed ovipositor. Like Tettigoniidae, both sexes have 'ears' on the forelegs and males have sound-producing organs on the forewings. The forewings fold in a box-like shape over the body. Sound production is very well developed and complex, calls being used to attract females and establish territories. Most species are nocturnal and omnivorous, often living in burrows or rock cracks.

### Common garden cricket
*Gryllus bimaculatus*

**length 25mm** Large, shiny and black with 2 pale yellow shoulder patches. **BIOLOGY:** Call is loud and familiar, softening when the cricket is approached. Male is aggressive and often kills competitor males. Large numbers gather around lights. **HABITAT:** Ubiquitous in the region and occurs across Africa, Europe and Asia, especially in association with human habitation. Always hides in cracks, crevices or beneath objects, especially where food is discarded.

### Tree crickets
*Oecanthus* spp.

**length 16mm** Fragile; pale green or straw-coloured; wings translucent; females have a short ovipositor. **BIOLOGY:** Call a pure, tremulous, musical chirp heard on still evenings. Call changes with temperature; for a known species one can determine night temperature by the chirp rate (hence they are also known as thermometer crickets). Eggs laid in slits in stems. Adults feed on young shoots, aphids and caterpillars. **HABITAT:** Widespread; abundant in grassland.

**CRICKETS AND THEIR RELATIVES**

### Mole crickets
Family Gryllotalpidae

**length 25–30mm** 3 spp. in SA; recognized by cylindrical, furry, light brown body, and enlarged forelegs, adapted for burrowing. Forewings are scales, hindwings are pleated and folded, with tips like spikes. **BIOLOGY:** Males produce penetrating, buzzing calls from a 1m-deep, forked burrow. Feed on plant roots and plant tissue; may be pests. *Gryllotalpa africana* (shown, length 30mm) occurs across Africa. **HABITAT:** Wet grassland; lawns in suburbs.

### Pygmy mole crickets
Family Tridactylidae

**length 5mm** 2 genera, *Tridactylus* and *Xya* (shown) in SA. Small, cylindrical, shiny black, rarely brown, with reduced forewings and long hindwings. Forelegs strong, for burrowing, hindlegs powerful, with large, flattened spurs. **BIOLOGY:** Excavate shallow burrows like welts across the ground and feed on microbes. Prodigious jumpers, using spurs for leverage; can jump off the water surface. Swim well. **HABITAT:** Seepages and the shores of water bodies.

### Groundhoppers
Family Tetrigidae

**length 7–12mm** ± 25 spp. in SA; small, dull-coloured and grasshopper-like, but with a hood-like pronotum extending to end of the body (not end of thorax). Forewings reduced to small scales, but hindwings large and fan-like in species capable of flight. *Tetiella* sp. (shown, length 12mm) is stocky, flightless, with a curved pronotal shield. **BIOLOGY:** Feed on surface algal films. **HABITAT:** Common in flooded grassland, vleis and wetland margins.

### Bush hoppers
Family Euschmidtiidae

**length 20–24mm** 8 spp. in SA; small; many are short-winged or wingless; antennae short. *Amatonga* sp. (shown) medium-sized, with cylindrical body tapering at both ends; green or brown, with a white cheek stripe. Rests with hindlegs wide apart. **BIOLOGY:** Many bush hoppers live on plants and shrubs, sitting with the hindlegs positioned at 90 degrees to the body, and body flat on the substrate. Food plants varied. **HABITAT:** Normally shrubs.

**CRICKETS AND THEIR RELATIVES**

### Bladder grasshoppers

Family Pneumoridae
**length 44–86mm** Virtually endemic, with 17 spp. in SA; large, usually bright green, arboreal. Pronotum inflated, especially in nymphs. *Bullacris intermedia* (length 45mm) shown. Male Pneumoridae have very large, broad forewings, shorter hindwings and an abdomen that acts as a resonating chamber. Females with reduced wings hidden by pronotum. Hindlegs not enlarged. **BIOLOGY:** Mating calls travel far. Feed on a few host plants. **HABITAT:** Forest; some occur in drier areas.

### Shield-backed locusts
Family Pamphagidae
**length 35–100mm** > 70 spp. in southern Africa, half of them endemic. Primitive, heavily built, large grasshoppers, normally cryptically coloured in dull earthy shades, or superbly camouflaged to mimic stone. When viewed from above, snout region of the head has a short furrow running toward the eyes (the 'fastigial furrow'). Antennae very broad and sword-shaped, triangular (not round) in cross section. Body surface very rough, often bearing tubercles and spines. Pronotum has raised, keel-like crest, which may be punctured with a series of small holes. Males usually winged and females commonly wingless. Most males are able to stridulate, using various mechanisms.

### Rain locusts
*Lamarkiana* spp.

**length 60–100mm** 20 spp. in SA; generally uniform grey with very flattened antennae, a cream cheek and prothoracic stripe and smoky-black hindwings. **BIOLOGY:** Males sluggish, nocturnal, winged and call from trees and shrubs; females wingless and rest on the ground. When flushed, males fly strongly for some distance. **HABITAT:** Various low, sparse vegetation types in semiarid areas.

### Stone grasshoppers
*Trachypetrella* spp.
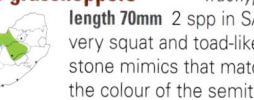

**length 70mm** 2 spp in SA; large, very squat and toad-like. Superb stone mimics that match both the colour of the semitranslucent pinkish-white quartz stones among which they live, but also the texture, including the chipped fracture planes. Wings vestigial; thin antennae can be withdrawn into sockets. Legs have border of hairs that blend with the body when they are withdrawn. **BIOLOGY:** When molested, they lash out the hindlegs with strength and speed, generating a grating sound. **HABITAT:** Quartz plains with little vegetation.

# Foam grasshoppers (lubber grasshoppers)     Family Pyrgomorphidae

**length 20–75mm** 39 spp. in SA; small to large grasshoppers distinguished by the combination of bright colours, a conical head and a pair of warty crescents on either side of the 'fastigial furrow' (which runs from the snout towards eyes). Many have warning coloration and are capable of producing a foamy defensive secretion; a few produce sounds. Most feed on herbs or shrubs, rarely on grasses. Many species are gregarious at all stages.

## Green milkweed locust    *Phymateus viridipes*

**length 70mm** Forewings and body green; hindwings blue and red. Nymph shiny black and gregarious. **BIOLOGY:** Like most *Phymateus* spp., raises the wings and rustles them when alarmed, then produces evil-smelling foam from the thoracic joints. In late summer, flies strongly and at some height, forming swarms of many thousand individuals and migrating long distances. **HABITAT:** Common in the summer-rainfall region, usually in areas with stands of its host plant, the milkweed *Asclepias fruticosus*.

## Koppie foam grasshopper
*Dictyophorus spumans*

**length 64mm** Heavily built with shortened forewings, hindwings absent; body mostly black, with 'sealing wax'-red patches on thorax and legs. Abdomen banded in black and white. **BIOLOGY:** Retains heart poisons (cardiac glycosides) from its food plants (various milkweeds of the family Asclepiadaceae). **HABITAT:** Occurs in areas of low vegetation, typically on koppies.

## Elegant grasshopper    *Zonocerus elegans*

**length 28–50mm** Brightly coloured body with yellow, black and blue markings; shortened forewings reddish. Eyes and antennae orange. **BIOLOGY:** Feeds on a range of plants, including the toxic Bitter apple *Solanum panduriforme* and various crops; may become a pest. **HABITAT:** Common in grassland and open woodland. Invades agricultural and disturbed land.

## Short-horned grasshoppers and locusts
Family Acrididae

**length 15–90mm** Diverse; with nearly 400 spp. in SA. Contains typical grasshoppers and locusts. All adults are winged, with short antennae and a hearing organ ('tympanum') on either side of the abdomen. Female's egg-laying tube ('ovipositor') is hidden inside the body, but can be extruded when she lays her frothy egg packages in the soil. These packages later harden and can endure long periods of drought. They typically feed on grasses, often competing with cattle and antelope. Males call by rubbing a file-like part of the hindleg against part of the forewing.

### Common stick grasshopper
*Acrida acuminata*

**length 66mm** Familiar, large green grasshopper, which reveals pale yellow or purplish hindwings when in typical skipping flight. Generates a crackling sound in flight. Top of head is elongated and bears long, flattened antennae. Egg pod very elongated; nymph green and very thin. **BIOLOGY:** Adults present in late summer, feeding on both soft and hard grasses. **HABITAT:** Usually in sandy areas in various vegetation types, often along river banks.

### Brown locust
*Locustana pardalina*

**length 40–50mm** Occurs in 2 forms. The larger, gregarious or migratory form is yellow, with very long wings peppered with black spots from about halfway along their length to their tips. Hindwings pale blue. Smaller, solitary form has green body marked with brown and black. Nymphs black and orange, gregarious. **BIOLOGY:** Major agricultural pests in the Karoo when numbers build up after heavy summer rains. **HABITAT:** Semiarid parts of the Karoo; swarms may extend into other parts of the region.

### Garden locust
*Acanthacris ruficornis*

**length 65 mm** Familiar tan locust with a white stripe running along the length of the body, and white spines on the hindlegs. Hindwings pale yellow. In contrast to adults, nymphs soft-bodied and light green. **BIOLOGY:** Rests and feeds on trees and shrubs, occasionally also eating grasses. Very large eggs laid in a flimsy egg case in loose soil. **HABITAT:** Moist habitats, including gardens and cropland; rare in semiarid areas.

### Desert locust
*Schistocerca gregaria*

**length 72mm** Body greenish-white in solitary phase, becoming yellowish in swarming phase. Pronotum has 3 longitudinal cream stripes. Eyes with vertical stripes. Forewings very long with white wing veins, hindwings pale yellow. **BIOLOGY:** Rarely swarms in South Africa, even though swarming phase does occur. A major pest in North Africa. **HABITAT:** Arid parts of the region; absent from high-rainfall zones; may swarm along the Orange River.

### Canary grasshoppers
*Heteracris* spp.

**length 30mm** Have striking yellow-and-black-banded hindlegs and a bright yellow mask surrounding the large black eyes. Antennae very long. **BIOLOGY:** Agile and alert, perching briefly on rocks and twigs. **HABITAT:** Grasses and herbs in dense riverine forest in warmer parts of the region.

### Common redleg grasshopper
*Orthoctha dasycnemis*

**length 22mm** Body green, with brown-edged, tan longitudinal stripe. Legs reddish brown, fading to green where they join the body. Antennae long and dark brown. **BIOLOGY:** Eggs hatch after first summer rains, only 1 generation per year. Feeds on both tough and soft grasses, including the Common bristle grass *Setaria sphacelata*. **HABITAT:** Dense, tall grass.

### Burrowing grasshoppers
*Acrotylus* spp.

**length 20–30mm** Cryptic brown and tan, hindlegs with black bands, midlegs adapted for digging, eyes bulging. Hindwing red or blue, with a black border. **BIOLOGY:** Partially bury themselves when wind picks up. When disturbed, make short flights, displaying colourful hindwings. Two generations per year. *A. patruelis* (shown) is among most common grasshoppers in SA. **HABITAT:** *Acrotylus* spp. favour sandy areas, including agricultural land and homesteads.

**CRICKETS AND THEIR RELATIVES**

### Blue wing
*Sphingonotus scabriculus*

**length 24–32mm** Coloration very cryptic, usually slate grey with 4 darker bands along tegmina, but varies to match stones on substrate. Hindwings bright blue at their base, with broad black border. **BIOLOGY:** Flight buoyant. When disturbed, makes snapping sound in flight, displaying black hindwings. **HABITAT:** Stony substrates (like shale or limestone) in arid parts.

### Yellow wings
*Oedaleus* spp.

**length 28–42mm** Abdomen yellow, tegmina boldly banded in black and tan, thorax with a pair of white stripes along each side and prothorax with thin white chevron markings. Hindwings banded bright yellow and black. **BIOLOGY:** They lay curved and constricted egg pods in very hard soils and produce 2 generations per season. Feed on short grasses. Males emit a crackling noise in flight. **HABITAT:** Open areas where the grass is very short, including overgrazed pasture – avoid tall grasses.

## WEBSPINNERS
**Order Embiidina (Embioptera)**

Small (length 5–20mm), poorly known order of cryptic insects that construct silken tunnels, which are hidden under bark, rocks, grass tufts or in soil. Females wingless, males may have smoky black wings and are attracted to lights. Live in groups, with nymphs inhabiting the same burrow as their parents. The tarsi on the forelegs are swollen with silk glands.

### Saunders' webspinner
*Oligotoma saundersii*

**length 7mm** An invasive dark brown species with winged males. The latter resemble small termites with smoky grey wings. **BIOLOGY:** Males, females and young live together in the same silk tunnels, from which they emerge at night to feed on lichen and algae. Males fly to lights at night. **HABITAT:** Trunks of trees in urban areas, often along roadsides.

# HEELWALKERS
**Order Mantophasmatodea**

Small order, discovered only in 2002, with ± 20 spp. in 3 families; many undescribed. Medium-sized, nocturnal, with egg, nymph and adult stage, but no pupa (i.e. 'hemimetabolous'). Superficially resemble mantid nymphs. Fore- and midlegs adapted for capturing small insect prey. Antennae have alternating long and short segments and end in a large hook. Tarsus is held off the ground, hence common name.

## Southern heelwalkers
**Family Austrophasmatidae**

**length 10–20mm** ± 10 spp. in SA. Small to medium-sized, largely restricted to the more arid parts of the winter-rainfall region. Eyes generally mottled with pigment, except for *Viridiphasma*, which has a striped eye. Blunt claspers (modified cerci) at end of the male's abdomen are used for grasping females during mating.

### Green heelwalker
*Viridiphasma clanwilliamense*

**length 11mm** Female plain jade green, male yellow-green, with brown stripe running along length of the body. Eyes yellow with a red stripe. **BIOLOGY:** As with all heelwalkers, mating lasts for up to 2 days; female often devours male thereafter. Nymphs grow in winter, adults present in spring. **HABITAT:** Camouflaged in tall shrubs and trees in mountain fynbos.

### Namaqualand heelwalker
*Karoophasma biedouwense*

**length 14–20mm** Colour variable, straw yellow to grey. Eye grey and mottled. Male smaller and more slender than female, which has a swollen abdomen. **BIOLOGY:** Egg pods are laid in a sand capsule hardened with body secretions; hatch after first autumn rains, but can remain dormant in the event of drought. **HABITAT:** Spiny bushes in arid fynbos and succulent karoo.

### Fynbos heelwalker
*Austrophasma redelinghuysense*

**length 11–18mm** Light brown with dark central stripe along the body in sand plain fynbos populations; bright green with a central pinkish stripe in mountain fynbos forms. **BIOLOGY:** Both sexes duet by rapidly tapping the substrate; males have tapping plate beneath the tip of the abdomen. **HABITAT:** Low vegetation; hides by day in the culms at the base of a restio.

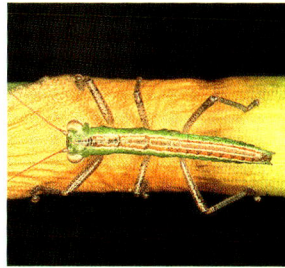

# STICK INSECTS
**Order Phasmatodea**

Easily recognized, large, elongate insects, known for mimicking twigs or leaves (hence the name, derived from Greek *phasma* = 'phantom'). Wings present or absent, females often larger, more robust and more numerous than males. All are herbivorous and most are nocturnal. Large, hard, seed-like eggs are simply dropped to the ground or are attached to the substrate. After 20–30 days nymphs emerge and moult 6–7 times, over several months, before reaching adult size.

## Common walking sticks
Family Heteronemiidae

**length 70–250mm** Diverse, cosmopolitan family including the largest and most spectacular stick mimics, but with only 5 spp. in SA. Sexes differ in form, with males usually winged.

### Giant stick insect
*Bactrododema tiaratum*

**length 110–250mm** Among the largest spp. in SA; dark brown, with rough texture and 2 spikes on top of the head. Female robust, wingless; male much smaller, with fully developed wings and wing membrane marked with brown bands. **BIOLOGY:** Males may flash wings in threat display. Sometimes attracted to lights. **HABITAT:** Trees and shrubs, especially in warmer areas.

## Bacillid stick insects
Family Bacillidae

**length 40–70mm** An African and Mediterranean group of stick insects with 5 spp. in SA. Both males and females are slender and wingless.

### Thunberg's stick insect
*Macynia labiata*

**length 42–56mm** Female large, plump, light green with cream to red longitudinal band; head and mouthparts pink to red. Male smaller, slender, brownish green, with reddish terminal cerci for grasping female when mating. Both sexes wingless. **BIOLOGY:** Dark brown eggs hatch after 4–6 months, nymphs mature in 6 months. Breed October–January, then die. **HABITAT:** Mainly Australian myrtle and *Erica* spp.

### Grass stick insect
*Maransis gramineus*

**length 61mm** Wingless; pale brown with red or dark brown stripe along both body and head, legs usually green at base. Female stout; male extremely delicate with very elongate forelegs and hook-like terminal cerci. **BIOLOGY:** Difficult to spot among the drying grass on which it feeds. **HABITAT:** Grassland.

# PSOCIDS (BOOKLICE)
**Order Psocoptera**

Diverse group of mostly small, soft-bodied, cryptic insects with large, round heads, long, slender antennae and (usually) large eyes. Most have delicate, transparent wings held in a characteristically tilted, roof-like position over the body, but some are wingless. They feed on algae, lichens, fungi and plant debris, or in the case of the introduced domestic species, on stored products. Although common on bark, in leaf litter and under rocks, they are easily overlooked. Often referred to as 'booklice', but are neither parasitic nor closely related to true lice (p.46), so the common name 'psocids' is preferred.

## Booklice
Family Liposcelidae

**length 1–2mm** Tiny, wingless, plain brown insects with flattened bodies and enlarged heads bearing small eyes. Bases of third pair of legs distinctively enlarged. The domestic booklouse *Liposcelis bostrychophila* (shown) is introduced. **BIOLOGY:** It is associated with paper and stored products in warm, damp habitats, can cause damage to documents and spoilage of food products and may cause allergic reactions. Best controlled by reducing humidity. **HABITAT:** It frequents dwellings throughout the region.

## Common barklice
Family Psocidae

**length up to 5mm** 12 spp. in SA, among which are most of the large species of psocid; superficially grey or black, but many have beautifully patterned wings. *Psococeratis* sp. (shown, length 4mm) is a tropical, solitary form. **BIOLOGY:** In some species, nymphs, or mixed nymphs and adults, form aggregations on tree trunks, scattering when disturbed and then reforming. They feed mostly on lichens. **HABITAT:** Most are associated with bark.

## Hairy psocids
Family Amphipsocidae

**length 5mm** Attractively mottled in white and brown, with broad wings that are held in a more horizontal posture than is typical of other psocids. Main veins of the wings are lined by double rows of setae; wing margins are lined by shorter setae. *Harpezoneura multifurcata* (shown) is the only named species in the region. **BIOLOGY:** Habits not known. **HABITAT:** Leaves of trees.

# LICE

**Order Phthiraptera**

Small, wingless insects with reduced eyes, short antennae and short, stout legs that end in strong claws. All are obligate external parasites of birds and mammals, and many are specific to a single host; indeed, some host species house several different lice, each confined to different parts of the body! Entire life cycle takes place on the host. Eggs are cemented to the host's feathers or hair and hatch into nymphs that moult three times before reaching maturity. Most lice live 30–40 days. Some are of medical significance, or are responsible for production losses in livestock industries.

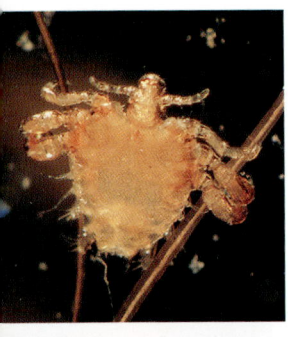

## Pubic lice (crab lice)    Family Pthiridae

**length 1–2mm** Tiny lice with characteristic rounded, flattened bodies and crab-like appearance. Have strong claws to grip pubic hair. Human pubic louse *Pthiris pubis* (shown) is the only species in the region. **BIOLOGY:** Human species spread by sexual contact or shared clothing. Eggs ('nits') attached to pubic hair. Life cycle 16–25 days. Feed exclusively on blood, the saliva causing irritation. **HABITAT:** Human pubic hair, rarely on the coarse hairs of the beard, armpits or eyelashes.

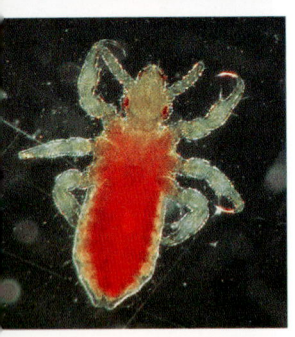

## Human lice    Family Pediculidae

**length 2–3mm** Tiny, wingless insects with elongate abdomen and all 3 pairs of legs equally developed, each ending in a strong claw. Head louse *Pediculus humanus capitis* (shown) is the only common species in the region. **BIOLOGY:** Feeds exclusively on blood. Its eggs ('nits') are attached to hair shafts, particularly behind the ears. Easily spread by bodily contact or shared combs and brushes and particularly common in children. Not a disease vector, but can cause itching. **HABITAT:** Humans.

## Biting bird lice    Family Menoponidae

**length 2–12mm** Diverse, with >300 spp. in SA. Identified by short antennae concealed in grooves behind the eyes. Includes the common chicken louse *Menopon gallinae*. **BIOLOGY:** Some bite holes in the quills of feathers and live inside the shaft. One genus lives inside the throat pouches of cormorants and pelicans! Largely host-specific. **HABITAT:** Exclusively parasitic on birds, crawling among, and feeding on, feathers; occasionally sucking blood.

# BUGS
### Order Hemiptera

One of the largest orders of insects, with thousands of species in SA. Highly variable in size, appearance and habits. May have wings; legs may be modified for jumping, swimming or walking. All bugs possess piercing-and-sucking mouthparts, which typically form an elongate 'beak' folded back between the front legs. Most feed on the sap of plants, but some feed on the body fluids of animals. Many are significant agricultural pests or vectors of diseases, but some play a beneficial role by controlling pests. Nymphs are smaller, wingless versions of the adults.

## Bed bugs
### Family Cimicidae

**length 4–5mm** ± 10 spp. in SA; small, oval, flattened brown ectoparasites. Forewings reduced to pads, hindwings absent. Best known species is the human bed bug *Cimex lectularius* (shown). **BIOLOGY:** It is extremely cryptic; hides by day, emerging at night to feed on human blood. Its saliva contains painkillers and anticoagulants so bites may go unnoticed, but can cause swelling, irritation and allergic reactions. Is not known to transmit pathogens. May leave blood spots on sheets, moulted exoskeletons and a smell of rotting raspberries! **HABITAT:** Bedding, clothing and crevices in furniture and walls.

## Plant or capsid bugs
### Family Miridae

**length 2–12mm** Very diverse, with >250 spp. in SA; small, fragile, terrestrial bugs. Body usually oval to elongate; may be drab or brightly coloured; some are ant mimics. *Stenotus* (shown, length 12mm) contains several of the larger, more conspicuous species. **BIOLOGY:** *Stenotus* spp. feed on grasses. **HABITAT:** Almost any type of vegetation.

## Lace bugs
### Family Tingidae

**length 2–7mm** ± 200 spp. in SA; body broad, usually dorsoventrally flattened, easily recognized by intricate lace-like patterning on the wings and thorax. The introduced Sycamore tree lacebug *Corythucha ciliata* (length 2.5mm) is shown. **BIOLOGY:** This species pierces the cells of host trees, sucks the sap and can be a significant pest; damaged leaves look bronzed and fall early. Overwinters under bark. **HABITAT:** It is restricted to suburban plane trees, *Planatus acerifolia*.

### Assassin bugs
Family Reduviidae

**length 7–27mm** Diverse, with 475 spp. in SA; quite robust, with powerful recurved beaks. Tip of the beak can be rubbed against a ventral groove, producing a sound that may aid species recognition. Some *Rhinocoris* spp. (like that shown) are brightly coloured. **BIOLOGY:** Stealthy ambush predators, injecting paralyzing saliva and sucking out the victim's body fluids. Handle carefully, as bites are painful. **HABITAT:** Diverse, often in bush or under stones.

### Ambush bugs
Subfamily Phymatidae

**length 7–15mm** 2 spp. in SA; distinct, stout, often cryptic bugs characterized by a strongly dilated abdomen, powerful front legs and thickened antennae, with the last segment swollen. An unidentified *Narina* sp. shown (length 10mm). **BIOLOGY:** Diurnal predators, lying in wait on flowering plants to seize visiting pollinating insects, such as bees, wasps or flies. Can take prey considerably larger than themselves. **HABITAT:** Both species associated with fynbos.

### Stilt bugs
Family Berytidae

**length 5mm** Small in size, so poorly known, with only 15 spp. in SA. *Metacanthus* sp. shown. Stilt bugs are small, delicate, with extremely long legs and antennae. Antennae 4-segmented, the last segment expanded into a club; swollen femora give knob-kneed appearance. **BIOLOGY:** Stilt bugs feed mostly on grasses and shrubs, but some species reportedly feed on small insects, like aphids. **HABITAT:** Grasses and trees.

### Flat bugs (bark bugs)
Family Aradidae

**length 2–12mm** ± 55 spp. in SA; *Strigocoris* sp. shown. Flat bugs are cryptic, dull-coloured, with short, stout legs. Best identified by their broad, flattened bodies and habitat. **BIOLOGY:** Feed on wood-decaying fungi. Some species guard their eggs until they hatch. **HABITAT:** Under loose bark on dead branches or trees.

## Leaf-footed bugs and twig-wilters
Family Coreidae

**length 7–36mm** Diverse, with ± 150 spp. in SA; medium-sized to large, with at least 7 conspicuous veins on the forewing covers, a stink gland between the mid- and hindlegs, and often enlarged or lobed hindlegs. *Holopterna alata* shown (length 23mm). **BIOLOGY:** Feed on shoots, seeds or fruit, some species causing characteristic wilting of shoots. Some are agricultural pests. **HABITAT:** Specific host plants.

## Broad-headed bugs
Family Alydidae

**length 14–19mm** 25 spp. in SA; medium-sized, mostly dull brown and easily recognized by slender body, broad, triangular head and enlarged hindlegs. The final antennal segments are elongated and curved. *Mirperus jaculus* shown (length 14mm). **BIOLOGY:** Broad-headed bugs feed on seeds and may gather in large numbers under trees, where seed pods have fallen. In some species, nymphs are ant mimics. **HABITAT:** *M. jaculus* frequents grasses.

## Cotton stainers
Family Pyrrhocoridae

**length 5–20mm** 35 spp. in SA; often brightly coloured in red, yellow and black. Frequently encountered as mating pairs, attached by the tails, or as aggregations of adults and nymphs. *Dysdercus* sp. shown (length 17mm). **BIOLOGY:** Cotton stainers feed mostly on ripe or developing seeds, but also on stems. **HABITAT:** *Dysdercus* spp. are pests of cotton, damaging the seeds and transmitting a fungus that stains the cotton yellow or brown.

## Seed bugs
Family Lygaeidae

**length 12–14mm** Diverse; some 400 spp. in SA; medium-sized, slender to oval, with 4–5 simple longitudinal veins on the forewing covers (cf. Coreidae, above, which have 7). Some are plain brown, others, like the Milkweed bug *Oncopeltus famelaris* (shown, length 14mm), are strikingly marked in black, yellow and orange. **BIOLOGY:** Seed bugs can be significant pests in gardens and agriculture. **HABITAT:** *O. famelaris* frequents granadillas and sweet potatoes.

### Burrowing bugs
Family Cydnidae

**length 4–15mm** ± 30 spp. in SA; medium-sized, shiny, oval, dark brown to black bugs with tough bodies. Mid- and hindlegs have close combs of stiff spines. *Geocnemis plagiata* (length 11mm) shown. **BIOLOGY:** Some feed on plant stems, but most occur underground, piercing the roots or other subterranean parts of plants and sucking the sap. May congregate around lights at night. **HABITAT:** In soil or under stones and leaves around plants.

### Pill bugs
Family Plataspidae

**length 9–13mm** 25 spp. in SA; very broad, strongly convex, dome-shaped bugs, usually dull in colour. The 'scutellum', a shiny extension to the thorax, is greatly enlarged, covering the whole abdomen and the long, folded wings. *Libyaspis wahlbergi* (length 12mm) shown. **BIOLOGY:** Most species suck sap from plants in the pea family (Leguminaceae), but some are thought to feed on fungi beneath the bark. **HABITAT:** Host plants.

### Shield-backed bugs
Family Scutelleridae

**length 6–20mm** ± 30 spp. in SA; oval to elongate; recognized by the massively enlarged extension to the thorax ('scutellum'), which covers the abdomen and wings. Some vaguely resemble beetles; many with brilliant metallic hues (hence also known as jewel beetles). *Calidea dregii* (length 14mm) shown. **BIOLOGY:** Feed on a range of shrubs and grasses. May release defence chemicals when disturbed. **HABITAT:** Host plants. Most diverse in tropical regions.

### Inflated stink bugs
Family Tessaratomidae

**length 15–30mm** ± 10 spp. in SA; quite large, with a flattened, expanded abdomen; usually yellow or green. Extension to thorax ('scutellum') is triangular and reaches middle of the (often laterally expanded) abdomen. *Encosternum delegorguei* (length 25mm) shown. **BIOLOGY:** These bugs suck juices from shrubs and trees. Can secrete noxious protective chemicals with some force. May form huge swarms. A local delicacy. **HABITAT:** Trees and shrubs in tropical areas.

## False stink bugs (shield bugs)
Family Acanthostomatidae

**length 5–20mm** A minor family. Flattened, mostly brown or streaked, distinguished from true stink bugs (Pentatomidae, below) by having 2 instead of 3 tarsal segments. The *Coenomorpha* sp. shown (length 20mm) is typical. **BIOLOGY:** Some species show maternal care. Nymphs are covered with a powdery wax. *Coenomorpha* spp. feed on Brazilian pepper trees. **HABITAT:** Mostly on woody plants.

## Stink or shield bugs   Family Pentatomidae

**length 6–18mm** Diverse, with ± 300 spp. in SA. Vary greatly in shape, but all have distinct dorsal 'shield', which extends at least halfway along the abdomen. *Nezara viridula* (length 12mm) shown. **BIOLOGY:** All are armed with stink glands and feed on a variety of plants and, rarely, on soft-bodied insects. Some, such as the introduced *Nezara viridula*, are common garden and agricultural pests. **HABITAT:** Food plants, which vary by species.

## Shore bugs   Family Saldidae

**length 2–7mm** 3 genera and 8 spp. in SA; elongate, oval and flattened, with broad head and very large eyes. Body usually brown, often with subtle white or yellow markings. *Capitonisalda* sp. (length 5mm) shown. **BIOLOGY:** Shore bugs prey on other insects. Agile and hard to catch, they run rapidly and jump readily. **HABITAT:** Margins of water bodies.

## Spiny shore bugs   Family Leptopodidae

**length 5mm** Only 1 species, *Valleriola moesta* (length 2–5mm) in SA. Spiny shore bugs are small, elongate and dull-coloured, with large eyes protruding from the sides of the head; antennae long and very thin; legs elongate, the first pair spiny and more robust. **BIOLOGY:** Predatory; very active and difficult to catch. **HABITAT:** Usually along the banks of fast-flowing streams, flying swiftly from rock to rock.

### Velvet water bugs
Family Hebridae

**length 2–3mm** 5 spp. in SA; minute, stout, dark-coloured aquatic bugs covered with a layer of short, dense fur – hence their common name. May be winged, have shortened wings or be wingless, depending on species. *Hebrus* sp. (length 2mm) shown. **BIOLOGY:** Walk slowly over the water surface (not 'skating') and feed on small arthropods. **HABITAT:** On the surfaces of well-vegetated ponds, or clinging to moss or floating vegetation.

### Water-treaders
Family Mesoveliidae

**length 3mm** Tiny, fairly slender, pear-shaped, generally olive-green aquatic bugs with long legs and antennae and large eyes. In the local species, *Mesovelia vittigera* (shown, length 3mm), males are winged, females are wingless. Females have a long, toothed ovipositor for laying eggs in plant tissue. **BIOLOGY:** Water-treaders prey on small crustaceans and insect larvae or scavenge on insects trapped in the surface film. **HABITAT:** On water surface or floating vegetation.

### Water crickets
Family Veliidae

**length 4–5mm** ± 15 spp. in SA; small, stout-bodied, aquatic bugs, with thorax much wider than the tapering abdomen. *Rhagovelia* sp. (length 5mm) shown. **BIOLOGY:** Water crickets look and behave like the larger pond skaters (below), but have evenly spaced, much shorter legs. Mostly wingless, but winged forms occur. Feed on dead insects on the water surface and probably on underwater that they spear from the surface. **HABITAT:** Water surfaces.

### Pond skaters
Family Gerridae

**length 5–20mm** ± 15 spp. in SA; well known, with narrow, compact body and elongate legs with hairs that support them above the water. *Gerris swakopensis* (length 11mm) shown. **BIOLOGY:** Gerridae skate across the water surface at speed, propelled by the middle pair of legs. Forelegs detect the vibrations of struggling prey or signalling mates. Feed on insects that fall into the water; may gather in groups around larger prey. **HABITAT:** Water surfaces.

### Water measurers  Family Hydrometridae

**length 9–10mm** 6 spp. in SA; thin and elongate, somewhat like tiny stick insects. Eyes in the middle of the very long head. Usually wingless. *Hydrometra* sp. (length 9mm) shown. **BIOLOGY:** Feed on insects trapped on the water surface, or may spear live food, such as mosquito larvae. Sometimes feed in groups on larger prey. Eggs laid singly on objects at or just above the water surface. **HABITAT:** Still water surfaces; floating vegetation.

### Velvety shore bugs  Family Ochteridae

**length 3–6mm** ± 1–2 spp. in SA; flattened, oval, usually brown, sometimes with blue or yellow spots; hindlegs spiny. *Ochterus caffer* (length 5mm) shown. **BIOLOGY:** Velvety shore bugs prey on fly larvae and small insects, such as springtails. Adults run and fly rapidly. Nymphs sometimes venture under the water for short periods, scooping up sand with the forelegs and gluing it onto their backs for camouflage. **HABITAT:** Shores of rivers, lakes and ponds.

### Toad bugs  Family Gelastocoridae

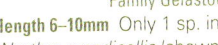

**length 6–10mm** Only 1 sp. in SA, *Nerthra grandicollis* (shown, length 5mm). Toad bugs are squat, robustly built and toad-like, with a broad, warty back, protuberant eyes and raptorial forelegs. They rarely fly; both winged and wingless species occur. **BIOLOGY:** They leap on and grasp insect prey with the enlarged forelegs. Nymphs cover themselves with sand. Males stridulate and females guard eggs. **HABITAT:** Margins of slow-flowing streams.

### Pygmy water boatmen  Family Micronectidae

**length 1–4mm** 1 genus, *Micronecta*, in SA, with 14 spp. of tiny, flat, oval, aquatic bugs, usually light brown, mottled and streaked with darker bands. Long hindlegs are fringed with hairs and held outstretched. **BIOLOGY:** Probably feed on bottom detritus. Males stridulate to attract females and defend territories. **HABITAT:** Still or slow-moving waters rich in oxygen, often in areas with little vegetation.

**BUGS**

### Water boatmen
Family Corixidae

**length 5–9mm** Only 14 spp. in SA, but an important family; flattened bugs with brown or black striations on thorax and wings; long hindlegs are fringed with hairs and stretched out sideways. Mouthparts short and conical. *Sigara* sp. (length 6mm) shown. **BIOLOGY:** Easily confused with backswimmers (below), but swim belly down, well below the surface, rising for air. Scoop up algae and detritus with the flattened forelegs; some eat fly larvae. **HABITAT:** Slow or stagnant waters.

### Backswimmers
Family Notonectidae

**length 4–12mm** Common family with 28 spp. in SA; aquatic, with pale (not striped), convex or keel-shaped dorsal surface. Mouthparts piercing; forelegs raptorial. *Anisops* sp. (length 11mm) shown. **BIOLOGY:** Swim head-down, but belly upward, near the surface, propelled by rapid strokes of the long, fringed hindlegs (cf. water boatmen, above). Active predators. Can inflict painful stab wound. Fly readily. **HABITAT:** Slow or stagnant waters; often in swimming pools.

### Pygmy backswimmers
Family Pleidae

**length 1.5–2.5mm** *Esakiella hutchinsoni* (shown, length 2.5mm) is the only species in SA; tiny, plump, humpbacked and aquatic. Legs short, with little modification for swimming. **BIOLOGY:** Swims well upside-down. Common but small; often escapes notice. Wings short; flight weak. Carries air in a felt-like cushion on the underside. Preys on small invertebrates. Both sexes produce sounds for communication. **HABITAT:** Clings to vegetation in still waters.

### Giant water bugs
Family Belostomatidae

**length 10–80mm** 7 spp. in SA; large, flattened, aquatic, light brown or green. Head conical, eyes large and projecting, often red. Forelegs adapted to capture prey, mid- and hindlegs flattened and fringed with hairs for swimming. *Lethocerus* sp. (length 60mm) shown. **BIOLOGY:** Fierce predators of tadpoles, fish and insects. Adults attracted to lights. Females sometimes glue eggs to the backs of males. **HABITAT:** Streams and ponds.

## Water scorpions
**Family Nepidae**

**length 20–45mm** 12 spp. in SA; large, aquatic; scorpion-like, elongate; breathing siphon may exceed length of the body (excluded from length given). *Laccotrephes* sp. (length 40mm) shown. **BIOLOGY:** Water scorpions hang from plants just below the water surface, breathe via their siphon and use the raptorial forelegs to grasp tadpoles, fish and invertebrates. Swim poorly, but can fly. Eggs laid in a tissue of aquatic plants. **HABITAT:** Plants in standing water.

## Saucer bugs
**Family Naucoridae**

**length 9–14mm** 9 spp. in SA; medium-sized, flattened, aquatic, with a short, sharp rostrum and well-developed forelegs, sometimes with greatly enlarged terminal 'claws'. Mid- and hindlegs fringed with hairs. *Laccoris* sp. (length 11mm) shown. **BIOLOGY:** Saucer bugs hunt for aquatic larvae. Some crawl through aquatic plants; others swim. Can inflict a painful sting. Females glue eggs to aquatic substrates. **HABITAT:** Ponds and mountain streams.

## Primitive snout bugs
**Family Cixiidae**

**wingspan 7–10mm** Diverse, very primitive family with 24 spp. in SA: small, relatively inconspicuous, with long faces, narrow heads and 3 simple eyes (in addition to compound eyes). Wings partly transparent, held in tent-like position over the body. *Inxwala modesta* (wingspan 14mm) shown. **BIOLOGY:** Adult Cixiidae eat woody vegetation; the nymphs eat underground roots. Some are pests of commercial crops. **HABITAT:** Bushveld and forest.

## Long-winged snout bugs
**Family Derbidae**

**length 16–24mm** Diverse, with 14 spp. in SA; easily identified by their oversized, delicate forewings, held upright above the body, and by their rudimentary hindwings. Eyes large and bulging. Wings and body often covered with a dusting of powdery wax. *Diostrombus abdominalis* (wingspan 16mm) shown. **BIOLOGY:** Adults suck sap, nymphs feed on fungi and mosses. **HABITAT:** Associated with palm trees; found underneath the leaves.

### Delphacid planthoppers
Family Delphacidae

**length 10mm** Diverse family, with 55 spp. of planthoppers in SA, but most are small and inconspicuous. Family members distinguished by the mobile spur on ends of the hindtibiae, but a microscope is needed to see this. *Perkinsiella saccharicida* (wingspan 14mm) shown. **BIOLOGY:** Feed on grasses. Some significant vectors of disease in maize, wheat and rice. *P. saccharicida* is an introduced pest of sugar cane. **HABITAT:** Subtropical grassland.

### Lantern bugs (snout bugs)
Family Fulgoridae

**length 15–30mm** Mostly tropical, with 22 spp. in SA; medium-sized to large, with some spectacular bugs with gaudy colours and/or bizarre, elongated snouts. Recognized by swollen first antennal segment and fan-like network of veins at the backs of the hindwings. *Zanna* sp. (length 31mm) shown. **BIOLOGY:** Suck sap through bark. Often cryptic, despite distinctive appearance. Nymphs covered with white wax. **HABITAT:** Bush and forest.

### Dictyopharid planthoppers
Family Dictyopharidae

**length 8–15mm** Diverse family, with 41 spp. in SA; small to medium-sized, often with a pointed snout; wings rather narrow, often clear and lacking the network of veins in the anal area typical of lantern bugs (above). Some species wingless. Usually green or brown. *Dictyophara* sp. (shown, wingspan 30mm) is typical, with a short snout and alert, upright posture. **BIOLOGY:** Feeds on sap. **HABITAT:** Grasses and herbaceous plants.

### Issid planthoppers
Family Issidae

**length 4mm** 19 spp. in SA; short, stocky, often dull brown or green, with short, hardened forewings that have pronounced ribs. Hindwings absent. Some local species have reduced, strap-like wings. *Johannesburgia* sp. (length 3mm) shown. **BIOLOGY:** Jump well. A bundled mass of straight, waxy filaments often projects from the rear in nymphs. Feeding poorly known. **HABITAT:** Scrubby vegetation; several unusual wingless species occur in fynbos.

## Tropiduchid planthoppers  Family Tropiduchidae

length 6–15mm  17 spp. in SA; medium-sized, greenish or brownish; body slender, head often pointed forward and wings held like a roof over the body. Nymphs have a tuft of wax filaments posteriorly. *Numicia insignis* (shown, length 12mm) has bright red eyes and a dark chevron pattern on the wings. **BIOLOGY:** Grass feeders; some are pests of sugar cane. **HABITAT:** Frequent grasses, usually in more tropical habitats.

## Eurybrachid planthoppers  Family Eurybrachidae

length 13–22mm  5 spp. in SA; medium-sized, head broad from above. Green, brown and grey blotches on forewings resemble bark and lichen; often has bright hindwings or abdomen (hidden beneath the wings), flashed in warning when disturbed. *Paropioxys jacundus* (shown, wingspan 26mm) is a bright, often-photographed lichen mimic that feeds on avocado and macadamia trees. **BIOLOGY:** Eurybrachidae feed on tree sap. **HABITAT:** Tree trunks.

A Weaving

## Moth bugs  Family Flatidae

length 10–15mm  ± 21 spp. in SA; moth-like, laterally flattened, wings broad, opaque, like a steep roof against the sides of the body and forming a peak. Yellow or green. Often in groups of adults and gregarious nymphs. Nymphs distinctive: body covered with curling filaments of white wax; sometimes called 'cotton bugs'. *Cryptoflata unipunctata* (wingspan 26mm) shown. **BIOLOGY:** Flatidae feed on vines, especially milkweed vines. **HABITAT:** Mostly in indigenous forest.

## Ricaniid planthoppers  Family Ricaniidae

length 6mm  10 spp. in SA; small, with attractively patterned wings, often banded in browns and blacks and with transparent windows. They spread their wings horizontally. Nymphs have posterior fans of wax filaments. *Mulvia albizona* (shown, wingspan 12mm) has 2 white transverse bands across the wings. **BIOLOGY:** Ricaniids feed on grasses and jump very well. **HABITAT:** Common in grasses growing in the shade of trees.

## Spittle bugs
Family Cercopidae

**length 15–40mm** 33 spp. in SA; nymphs live in a frothy ball of plant sap and air (hence the common name), to prevent drying out and to conceal them from predators and parasites. Adults stout, with large eyes and often bright red-and-black forewings. Most feed on grasses; excellent jumpers.

### Red-spotted spittle bug
*Locris arithmetica*

**wingspan 23mm** Common, bright red spittle bug with black markings. Nymphs concealed in a ball of spittle. Related *L. areata* has plain red wings. **BIOLOGY:** Adults usually seen feeding in small groups on the sap of Kikuyu grass, also on sugar cane. Common in urban areas. Nymphs are also sap feeders. **HABITAT:** Grasses.

### Rain-tree bug
*Ptyelus grossus*

**length 15mm** Adult with white head, slate-grey wings, each with white dots and 2 white patches. Nymph with orange central stripe and complex yellow-and-black markings. **BIOLOGY:** Gregarious; produces protective nests of foam. Copious sap dripping from dense aggregations of nymphs make wet patches on the ground, hence the name 'rain-tree bug'. **HABITAT:** Trees, often in urban areas.

### Cicadas
Family Cicadidae

**wingspan 30–90mm** Well-known, diverse family with ± 140 spp. in SA; adults robust, wings transparent, hindwings sometimes brightly coloured. *Platypleura* sp. (wingspan 60mm) shown. **BIOLOGY:** Cicada males call loudly; both sexes have ears on the underside of the abdomen. Nymphs live underground, feeding on roots. **HABITAT:** Trees; a few species on grasses or short vegetation.

### Treehoppers
Family Membracidae

**length 6–10mm** ± 120 spp. in SA; first thoracic segment forms a simple thorn-like extension or a branched structure extending over the abdomen. Bizarre, usually black, nymphs have elongate abdomens. *Oxyrachis* sp. (wingspan 18mm) shown. **BIOLOGY:** Suck sap and secrete honeydew, which is removed by attendant ants. **HABITAT:** Trees, shrubs and creepers.

## Leafhoppers
**Family Cicadellidae**

**length 2–10mm** Diverse; >300 spp. in SA, many endemic; small, often attractively coloured. Jump very well; hindtibiae lined with spines. Bodies coated with waxy granules thought to provide protection from predators and pathogens. *Poecilocarda cosmopolita* (wingspan 20mm) shown. **BIOLOGY:** Leafhoppers suck sap from one, or a related group of, hosts. Some are agricultural pests, damaging plants and transmitting viruses. **HABITAT:** Trees, shrubs and grasses.

## Jumping plant lice
**Family Psyllidae**

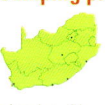

**length 1.5–5mm** Diverse, with 61 spp. in SA; tiny, usually dull; transparent wings have few, if any, cross veins. Resemble tiny cicadas. Nymphs flattened and may be covered with wax; some cause leaf galls. Blue gum psyillid *Retroacizzia mopanei* (wingspan 8mm) shown. **BIOLOGY:** Jumping plant lice are great jumpers, but weak fliers. A number, including the featured species, are significant plant pests. **HABITAT:** Usually on specific host trees.

## Triozid plant lice
**Family Triozidae**

**length 5mm** African citrus psylla *Trioza erytreae* (shown, wingspan 8mm) is best known: a tiny, delicate bug with alert, upright posture; easily mistaken for a fly. Initially pale, turns brown with age. Wings clear, extending well beyond the abdomen. Nymphs tiny, circular, with a fringe of waxy white filaments. **BIOLOGY:** Feeds on leaves, distorting shoots and transmitting greening disease. **HABITAT:** Citrus psylla occurs on citrus trees and related indigenous plants.

## Aphids
**Family Aphididae**

**length 1.5–5mm** Very diverse with >165 spp. in SA; well known, tiny, pear-shaped, soft-bodied. Wingless, or with clear wings. Can exude defensive fluid from abdomen. *Aphis nerii* (length 4mm) shown. **BIOLOGY:** Many are serious agricultural pests. Ants often 'milk' aphids for honeydew. Can give birth to live young asexually, or undergo sexual reproduction. Responsible for the transmission of many plant diseases. **HABITAT:** Host plants vary according to species.

### Whiteflies
Family Aleyrodidae

**length 2–4mm** ± 16 spp. in SA; resemble tiny moths; wings broad, some with red bands, held flat over abdomen; body and wings covered with white wax. Nymphs look like scale insects, immobile, covered in waxy white filaments; cluster under leaves. Recently introduced Woolly whitefly *Aleurothrixus floccosus* (wingspan 1mm) shown. **BIOLOGY:** Causes leaf drop in citrus. Honeydew from nymphs promotes sooty mould growth under leaves. **HABITAT:** Host plants.

### Armoured scale insects
Family Diaspididae

**length 1–2mm** Diverse, with 270 spp. in SA; strange, featureless, body concealed by an armoured 'scale' made of shed skins. Aloe red scale *Separaspis capensis* (length 1mm) shown. **BIOLOGY:** Armoured scale insects suck sap and do not produce honeydew, but their anal secretions may be used to bond scales together. Some are significant pests of citrus or other host plants. **HABITAT:** Firmly attached to the surfaces of leaves or fruit.

### Soft scale insects
Family Coccidae

**length 4–10mm** Large family, with 130 spp. in SA; females devoid of wings and sometimes legs; head, thorax and abdomen fused; body covered with a domed shield or amorphous cap like spilt candle wax. Males are typical winged insects. *Ceroplastes destructor* (diameter 10mm) shown. Females produce 'crawlers', which seek out new hosts. **BIOLOGY:** Soft scale insects produce honeydew; often attended by ants. Several are pests. **HABITAT:** Host plants.

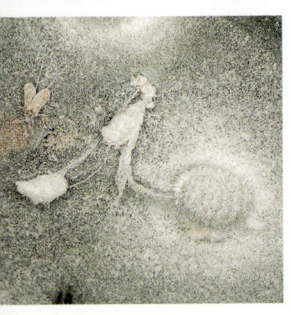

### Cochineal insects
Family Dactylopiidae

**length 2–3mm** 6 spp. in SA; males small, delicate, moth-like and winged, with 2 long tails. Females fat, soft-bodied and wingless, covered with waxy filaments. Cochineal bug *Dactylopius opuntiae* (length 3mm) shown. **BIOLOGY:** All cochineal insects were introduced to control cactus weeds or to make cochineal (± 100,000 *D. coccus* females produce a kilogram of this dye). **HABITAT:** On cactus species; congregate around the spines.

# THRIPS
### Order Thysanoptera

± 230 spp. in SA; minute insects with long, slender, cigar-shaped bodies and 2 pairs of narrow wings fringed with hair. Poor flyers, but are easily dispersed by wind. Most use their conical mouthparts to pierce plants and suck up their sap, but some are predatory on tiny arthropods, or feed on pollen, fungal spores or decaying plant matter. Extremely common, but are often overlooked because of their small size. Many are pests of commercial crops, damaging flowers or vegetables by their feeding activity and transmitting plant diseases, but they may also play positive roles as pollinators. The nymphs resemble wingless adults.

## Tube-tailed thrips
Family Phlaeothripidae

**length 2–4mm** Diverse group, with >100 spp. in SA, including winged and wingless species. Mostly dark in colour, with body distinctly depressed and the last abdominal segment characteristically modified into a tube-like structure (hence the common name). Wings are narrow and lack longitudinal veins. **BIOLOGY:** Most often seen feeding on pollen and frequently abundant in flower heads. Some are predatory, with strong, grasping forelegs. **HABITAT:** Flowers and leaves.

## Common thrips
Family Thripidae

**length 1–2mm** >100 spp. in SA; tiny, cryptic, often pale thrips, with flattened bodies and narrow wings with only 2 longitudinal veins. In females the last abdominal segment is divided to reveal a saw-like, downward-curving ovipositor. **BIOLOGY:** Some are significant pests, notably *Thrips tabaci*, which is an introduced pest of onions, tobacco, tomatoes and various other crops. **HABITAT:** Host plants.

## Banded thrips
Family Aeolothripidae

**length 2mm** Relatively small family with 13 spp. in SA; active, often dark, thrips, usually with conspicuously banded, spotted or striped forewings. Wings relatively broad and rounded at the tips, with 2 conspicuous longitudinal veins and several cross veins. Female has a saw-like ovipositor that curves upward (see Thripidae, above). **BIOLOGY:** Most feed on flowers, but some are obligate predators of mites. **HABITAT:** Usually on flowers.

# DOBSONFLIES AND ALDERFLIES
**Order Megaloptera**

Small order of medium-sized to very large insects, with <10 spp. in SA. Wings large, mottled grey to brown, and folded around the body at rest. Smaller simple eyes ('ocelli') occur between the large compound eyes. Veins reaching the front margin of the wing do not branch. Eggs are laid on marginal vegetation, hatching into larvae that drop into the stream. Carnivorous aquatic larvae ('toebiters') have large, stout jaws, gills fringing the abdomen, and feed on a range of aquatic insects and worms. They emerge to pupate in mud cells constructed among moss and stones along the river bank.

## Dobsonflies
Family Corydalidae

**wingspan 60mm** 11 spp. in SA; relatively large, lead-grey or brown insects. Wings extend beyond the tip of the abdomen at rest, wing veins dotted with dark spots. Larvae 40mm long with 8 pairs of gills along the length of the abdomen and a pair of hooks at the end. *Taeniochauliodes ochraceopennis* (shown) is the largest, commonest and most widespread species in SA; adults (top image) emerge November–February in the Western Cape. **BIOLOGY:** Large, slow-flying adults rest on marginal vegetation of mountain streams in summer; long-lived, fully aquatic larvae (bottom image) take years to develop. **HABITAT:** Fast-flowing, wooded mountain streams. Larvae occur under rocks; adults not far from water, usually in marginal vegetation.

## Alderflies
Family Sialidae

**length 8mm** Only 2 spp. in SA, both uncommon; adults very dark, almost black. Wings furled tightly around the body, as shown. Larvae (bottom image) slender, with 8 pairs of thin, unbranched gills along the abdomen, and with head and thorax marked in light and dark brown. Abdomen ends in a simple, long filament, not in a pair of hooks, as seen in dobsonfly larvae (above). **BIOLOGY:** *Leptosialis africana* (shown) occurs in the Western Cape. **HABITAT:** Much rarer than dobsonflies, alderflies occur in both fast-flowing mountain streams in the Western Cape and in sluggish, turbid rivers in KwaZulu-Natal.

# ANTLIONS AND LACEWINGS
**Order Neuroptera**

Order with 13 families and 400-odd spp. in SA. Adults have large wings with an intricate network of veins, and an elongated prothorax. Flight is weak and fluttering. They feed on pollen, nectar and other insects. Larvae are varied, but all have sucking mouthparts, often curved and toothed internally. Pupa forms in a silken oval cocoon and lacks an anus, so waste is stored as a white pellet excreted upon adult emergence.

## Dusty-winged lacewings
Family Coniopterygidae

wingspan 4–8mm  14 spp. in SA; very small; at rest, wings are held like a roof over the body; they are covered with a powdery, white waxy secretion and sometimes patterned with a few black dots. Antennae comprise long, bead-like segments. **BIOLOGY:** Widespread and beneficial, in that larvae feed on the eggs of insect pests as well as on scale insects and mites. **HABITAT:** Common and ubiquitous everywhere; also in gardens and agriculture.

## Brown lacewings
Family Hemerobiidae

wingspan 6–16mm  ± 22 spp. in SA; small, dull brown, wings often patterned and held like a steep roof over the body. Larvae slender and smooth, with long, thin, piercing mouthparts. *Micromus* sp. (wingspan 14mm) shown has narrow, plain brown wings. **BIOLOGY:** Adults attracted to lights. Adults and larvae are significant predators of aphids, other small sedentary insects, and their eggs. **HABITAT:** Common in most habitats, including gardens and orchards.

## Green lacewings
Family Chrysopidae

wingspan 15–50mm  ± 80 spp. in SA; green (rarely yellow, grey or red-marked) with broad, green wings held like a roof over the body. Eyes large and appear metallic. Larvae often long and green, with thin, elongated mouthparts. *Chrysoperla* sp. (shown, wingspan 24mm) is common in gardens and attracted to lights. **BIOLOGY:** Green lacewing adults and larvae feed on various bugs and their eggs and are useful in regulating insect pests on commercial crops and in gardens. **HABITAT:** Common in most vegetation types; adults often found on flowering trees.

## Spoonwing and threadwing lacewings
Family Nemopteridae

**wingspan 30–80mm** ± 60 spp. in SA. Adults have clear (rarely patterned) forewings and very elongated hindwings, either thread-like along their entire length (threadwing lacewings), or expanded and twisted terminally and banded (spoonwing lacewings). Mouthparts are extended into a beak ('rostrum'). Larvae live in fine sand in rock overhangs or in loose sand deposits.

### Threadwing lacewing
*Laurhervasia setacea*

**wingspan 25mm** Adults small-bodied and fragile, with iridescent forewings and thin white hindwings; males with small swelling along hindwings. Larvae with very long prothorax and curved jaws. **BIOLOGY:** Adults feed on pollen in summer; often attracted to lights. **HABITAT:** Fairly common in dry succulent karoo; larvae found on dry sand in rock overhangs.

### Rock spoonwing lacewing
*Palmipenna aeoleoptera*

**wingspan 32mm** Unmistakable, with large, dark brown, paddle-like expansions on hindwings (larger and darker in the male). Antennae stout; body brown above, yellow below. **BIOLOGY:** Adults active in spring, feeding on daisy and ice plant flowers using their probing rostrum. Males glide in courtship flight with the hindwings held together. Hindwings appear to reduce predation by robberflies. **HABITAT:** Only occur on a few, low-lying mountain slopes strewn with quartzitic rocks in succulent karoo vegetation.

### Beaded lacewings
Family Berothidae

**wingspan 12–20mm** ± 12 spp. in SA; similar to brown lacewings (p.63), but the forelegs of some species may be raptorial. *Podallea* sp. (wingspan 15mm) shown is quite common in woodland, has hooked wing tips, a hairy body and rests with antennae held together, head downward and body tilted upward. **BIOLOGY:** Larvae of family not known, but some suspected to live with and feed on termites. **HABITAT:** Fairly widespread, but rare.

# Mantidflies and mantispids
Family Mantispidae

**wingspan 12–60mm** ± 50 spp. in SA; medium-sized to large predators slightly resembling mantids. Forelimbs powerful and spined, prothorax elongated, head triangular with large eyes. Wings generally clear and glassy, with brown markings in those that mimic wasps, such as *Pseudoclimaciella* sp. (wingspan 38mm) shown. **BIOLOGY:** Stalked eggs laid in clusters, hatching into mobile larvae that seek out spider egg cases, where they feed on the eggs and developing spiderlings. **HABITAT:** Adults may be common on flowering trees, especially karee, *Rhus lancea*, and buffalo thorns, *Zizyphus* spp.

# Antlions
Family Myrmeleontidae

**wingspan 26–160mm** Medium-sized to very large; both adults and larvae predaceous. Larvae construct cone traps in sand, or live in loose sand and subdue prey with their stout, curved, toothed jaws. Adults may resemble dragonflies, but have stout, clubbed antennae.

## Gregarious antlion *Hagenomyia tristis*

**wingspan 70mm** Broad, iridescent blue wings with a white spot ('pterostigma') on the leading edge; body yellow with black markings and a stripe along the top of the abdomen. **BIOLOGY:** Characteristically form large swarms that fly weakly for a short distance when disturbed. **HABITAT:** Very common in dense grass under trees.

## Mottled veld antlion *Palpares caffer*

**wingspan 112mm** Very large; wings with yellow veins peppered with black dots, 3 indistinct black patches along their length. Body bright yellow with black markings, thorax furry. **BIOLOGY:** Often flushed and flies far before resettling. Attracted to lights. Large larvae live just below the surface of loose sand. **HABITAT:** Common, especially in grassland, right up to equatorial Africa.

### Owl flies
Family Ascalaphidae

**wingspan 44–80mm** ± 50 spp. in SA; adults resemble dragonflies, but with long, clubbed antennae. *Tmesibasis lacerata* (shown, wingspan 70mm) is unusual, with ornately patterned wings. Common name describes the forays of these insects hawking at dusk. Larvae oval, flattened, with lateral fringes and huge jaws held open at 180 degrees. **BIOLOGY:** Rest by day in a characteristic head-down posture. Flight rapid and low. **HABITAT:** A wide range of vegetation types in mesic and dry areas; fairly rare.

### Silky lacewings
Family Psychopsidae

**wingspan 10–22mm** 6 spp. in SA; unique, with exceptionally broad wings showing parallel venation. Wings mottled brown or grey, occasionally white and moth-like. Antennae and abdomen short, abdomen concealed under wings at rest. *Silveira jordani* (wingspan 17mm) shown. **BIOLOGY:** Fairly uncommon, and sometimes attracted to lights. Many rest on tree bark by day. Larvae predaceous with short jaws. **HABITAT:** Rare in subtropical forest, through open and arid woodland.

## BEETLES
**Order Coleoptera**

The most diverse order, making up nearly one-third of all known animal species and about 40% of all insects! Over 18,000 spp. in SA, ranging enormously in size, shape, ornamentation and colour and found in almost every terrestrial and freshwater habitat. Bodies hardened, forewings characteristically modified into tough, inflexible cases ('elytra'), meeting in the midline and protecting the membranous hindwings, which are used for flight. All have chewing mouthparts, but they may be herbivorous, predatory or parasitic.

### Reticulated beetles
Family Cupedidae

**length 18mm** Small family, with 1 sp. in SA, *Cupes capensis* (shown, length 18mm). Reticulated beetles are parallel-sided with a pattern of interconnecting longitudinal and transverse veins on the elytra – hence the common name. Usually brown or grey; antennae elongate and unusually thickened; eyes prominent. **BIOLOGY:** Larvae live in fungus-infected wood. Adults may be attracted to lights. **HABITAT:** Forests.

# Ground beetles

Family Carabidae

**length 5–55mm** Very large and diverse family with some 1,500 spp. in SA; mostly dull-coloured, somewhat flattened, predatory, ground-dwelling beetles. Head, thorax and abdomen are clearly differentiated; thorax is narrower than the elytra, which are often longitudinally grooved.

## Velvet ground beetles *Graphipterus* spp.

**length 10–14mm** Diverse, diurnal and predatory. Mandibles well developed, thorax relatively narrow, abdomen broadly oval, grooved longitudinally, legs long. Thorax and elytra covered with brownish hairs and often outlined with white, or patterned with black stripes (as in *G. trilineatus*, shown, length 12mm) or patches. **BIOLOGY:** Hunt actively, even in heat of the day. **HABITAT:** Open ground in arid areas.

## Burrowing ground beetle *Passalidius fortipes*

**length 32mm** Large and powerful, with fearsome, greatly thickened, pincer-like mandibles and powerful, strongly toothed tibiae on the forelegs. Body parallel-sided; elytra with marked longitudinal grooves. **BIOLOGY:** Burrow in soil in more arid parts of the region, hunting for termites and insect larvae on which to feed. **HABITAT:** Forests and savanna.

## Two-spotted ground beetle
*Anthia homoplatum*

**length 35mm** Large, active, long-legged; black with a distinctive pattern: elytra with 2 yellow spots on the front corners and a yellow line around the posterior margin. **BIOLOGY:** A diurnal predator. One of several similar species differing mainly in the colour and texture of the elytra (sometimes placed in the genus *Thermophilum*). **HABITAT:** Subtropical vegetation.

## Tyrant ground beetle *Anthia maxillosa*

**length 38mm** Large, conspicuous, formidable-looking beetle with extremely long, sharp mandibles; white hairs on first 3 antennal segments. Thorax characteristically dish-shaped. **BIOLOGY:** A fast-moving, diurnal predator, occurring in dry habitats. If molested can spray concentrated acid at the head and eyes of an attacker from up to 1m. **HABITAT:** Dry fynbos.

## Tiger beetles
Subfamily Cicindelinae

Distinctive, flattened, fast-running predatory beetles, with long legs and enlarged, curved mandibles. Some 150 spp. in SA, many with bright metallic colouring, or with distinctive geometric patterns on the elytra. Found mostly on bare ground.

### Common tiger beetle — *Lophyra brevicollis*

**length 17mm** Head and thorax copper, with scattered white hairs, face white, elytra yellow with characteristic geometric markings. A fast-running, predatory beetle with long, sharp, curved mandibles. **BIOLOGY:** Typically scurries around, flying for a few metres when disturbed. One of several species in the genus, each with slightly different colour patterns. **HABITAT:** Bare ground or sand, often near water.

### Emerald tiger beetle — *Cicindela quadriguttata*

**length 11mm** Relatively small; a distinctive metallic green colour; base of mandibles white; underside of body with white hairs; legs coppery. **BIOLOGY:** Diurnal, hunts for insects. Larvae ambush prey from within vertical burrows in flat ground, as do those of other tiger beetles. **HABITAT:** Near muddy pools in karoo and fynbos vegetation.

### Ants' nest beetles — Family Paussidae

**length 7–13mm** Diverse, with ± 85 spp. in SA; small to medium-sized, brown to red, with broad, flattened antennae and a remarkable association with ants. *Cerapterus curtisi* (body 7mm) shown. **BIOLOGY:** Paussidae eat ant larvae, pupae and adults. Secretions, especially from the antennae, induce ants to tolerate them. They produce a caustic, explosive chemical when disturbed. **HABITAT:** Ants' nests.

### Predaceous diving beetles — Family Dytiscidae

**length 10–45mm** Diverse, >300 spp. in SA. Common, smooth, oval, streamlined, aquatic beetles. The flattened, hairy hindlegs are used as paddles. *Cybister tripunctatus* (length 29mm) shown. **BIOLOGY:** Dytiscidae move their legs together, like oars (cf. water scavenger beetles, p.69). Rise tailfirst to replace air stored beneath the elytra. Adults and larvae are voracious predators. **HABITAT:** Most freshwater habitats.

## Water scavenger beetles
Family Hydrophilidae

**length 1–50mm** Diverse, ± 200 spp. in SA; mostly aquatic, small to large, usually shiny black or brown, with palps exceeding length of the short antennae. Unlike predaceous diving beetles (p.68), they swim using their legs alternately, and surface headfirst for air. *Hydrophilus* sp. (length 14mm) shown. **BIOLOGY:** Despite their name, they may be predatory or herbivorous. Larvae predatory. **HABITAT:** Fresh water or damp areas.

## Hister beetles
Family Histeridae

**length 1–20mm** ± 40 spp. in SA; most are shiny, oval and black; antennae elbowed with clubbed ends; elytra shortened, leaving last 2 abdominal segments exposed. Head usually deeply retracted into the prothorax. *Macrolister* sp. (length 8mm) shown. **BIOLOGY:** Most hister beetles are nocturnal and feed on dung, carrion and decaying matter or on other insects. Will play dead if threatened. **HABITAT:** Near dung or carrion; some live in ants' nests.

## Carrion beetles
Family Silphidae

**length 10–40mm** 3 spp. in SA; elongate, tapering, usually black or red, with weakly clubbed antennae and ribbed, shortened elytra leaving the last 1–4 abdominal segments exposed. *Thanatophilus mutilatus* (length 20mm) shown. **BIOLOGY:** Carrion beetles are known for their association with dead vertebrates; used in forensics to ascertain date of death. Larvae feed on carrion, adults also eat fly maggots. Can bury carcasses. **HABITAT:** Bird and mammal corpses.

## Rove beetles
Family Staphylinidae

**length 1–20mm** >750 spp. in SA; ancient and diverse; very small to medium-sized, brown to black. Narrow, elongate, with very short elytra leaving most of the abdomen exposed. *Dolicaon* sp. (length 18mm) shown. **BIOLOGY:** Rove beetles may run like earwigs, with the abdomen curled upward. Most prey on invertebrates or eat decaying plant and animal material. Some burrow below sand on beaches, eating microscopic algae. **HABITAT:** The ground.

### Cicada parasite beetles
Family Rhipiceridae

**length 12mm** Small family of specialized beetles with only ± 10 spp. in SA. Antennae prominent and fan-shaped; body mottled grey and covered with short hairs. **BIOLOGY:** Adults probably feed on pollen; sometimes attracted to lights. Larvae live underground and are external parasites of cicada nymphs. Little else is known of their biology. **HABITAT:** Adults visit flowers.

### Stag beetles
Family Lucanidae

**length 14–34mm** 22 spp. in SA; medium to large, usually black, with large, toothed mandibles and powerful digging forelegs. Cape stag beetle of genus *Colophon* (length 25mm) shown. **BIOLOGY:** *Colophon* has 17 endemic spp., each restricted to its own high-altitude mountain area and all endangered because of indiscriminate collecting and climate change. Larvae thought to feed on roots, and take 2 years to develop. Adults probably eat detritus. **HABITAT:** Mountain peaks.

### Carcass beetles
Family Trogidae

**length 5–15mm** ± 50 spp. in SA; grey to black with a downward-bent head largely concealed by the pronotum. Body surface covered with distinctive warty bumps and often encrusted with dirt. Legs adapted for burrowing. *Omorgus asperulatus* (length 15mm) shown. **BIOLOGY:** Trogidae are typically among the last to colonize the dry remains of dead animals. Both adults and the C-shaped white larvae feed on skin, fur and feathers. **HABITAT:** Animal carcasses and faeces.

### Dor beetles
Family Bolboceratidae

**length 10–25mm** ± 40 spp. in SA; globular, reddish to brown, with clubbed antennae, grooved elytra and broad front legs for digging. Some have horns on the head and pronotum. Underside covered with long hairs. *Meridiobolbus faustus* (length 15mm) shown. **BIOLOGY:** Dor beetles resemble dung beetles, also feeding on, and burying, dung to provision larvae. The larvae of some species eat grass roots and damage lawns and golf courses. **HABITAT:** Soil and dung.

## Scarab beetles
Family Scarabaeidae

**6–50mm** Very diverse family with >800 spp. in SA. Stout-bodied, medium-sized to large beetles, often black, but many with bright metallic colours. Highly variable in shape and habits, but best recognized by their distinctive antennae, which end in a club composed of 3–7 flat plates that can be compressed into a ball or fanned out like leaves to detect odours. Family includes many important and conspicuous species – some serious agricultural pests, others important as pollinators, or for their role in removing dung. Larvae are C-shaped, live underground and can also be pests.

## White-spotted fruit chafer
*Mausoleopsis amabilis*

**length 10–13mm** Distinctive black beetle with 4–5 large white patches and a few tiny white spots on each side. Several other similar white-spotted black species have more numerous, but smaller, spots. **BIOLOGY:** Adult *M. amabilis* are active September–May and frequently attracted to flowers, fruit or sap flows. Known to breed in goat and horse dung. **HABITAT:** Frequents subtropical forest and savanna.

## Garden fruit chafer
*Pachnoda sinuata*

**length 24mm** Adult shiny yellow with dark brown central area and yellow transverse stripe near tips of the elytra. **BIOLOGY:** Feeds on flowers, including roses and camellias, and on fruit trees, causing considerable damage to ripening fruit. Eggs are laid in compost heaps and hatch into large white grubs, which pupate in hard, egg-shaped protective cases. **HABITAT:** A familiar garden pest and the most common fruit chafer in the region.

## Green protea beetle
*Trichostetha fascicularis*

**length 25mm** Large, striking species with metallic green elytra; black head, and prothorax with 4 longitudinal white stripes. Underside and legs with prominent tufts of yellow hairs. **BIOLOGY:** Adults buzz noisily between flowers and bury themselves headfirst in blooms, feeding on pollen and nectar. Often transported with cut flowers and even reported from Germany in exported flowers. **HABITAT:** Always associated with *Protea* plants.

### Marbled fruit chafer  *Porphyronota hebreae*

**length 21mm** Yellowish brown, densely patterned with dark brown patches and spots, elytra with longitudinal grooves. **BIOLOGY:** Unusual in that adults are most commonly found feeding on exudates from damaged grass stems, although also recorded feeding on a variety of fruit and flowers. Active October–April, usually seen flying over grassland. Breeds in soil. **HABITAT:** Bushveld and grassland.

### Rose chafer  *Hypopholis sommeri*

**length 18mm** Head and pronotum dark brown, elytra lighter, with dark margins. **BIOLOGY:** Feeds nocturnally on the flowers and foliage of various crops and garden plants and commonly damages roses. Hides by day in leaf litter or soil. One of several similar brown chafers. Larva is a typical white grub that lives in soil. **HABITAT:** Forests, gardens and farmland.

### Blue monkey beetle  *Scelophysa trimeni*

**length 9–11mm** Male has enlarged hindlegs like other male monkey beetles; upper side of body covered with minute sky-blue scales, underside silvery. Female has thinner black legs with a few thick black hairs and ranges in colour from green to brown. **BIOLOGY:** Feeds on pollen from daisies and ice plants, often in groups buried headfirst in the disc of a flower. Larvae probably feed on roots. **HABITAT:** Sandy coastal areas.

### Large barred monkey beetle
*Monochelus niewoudtvillensis*

**length 10mm** Male brownish black with chequered black-and-white margins to the abdomen and with black legs, the hind pair enlarged; female is covered with orange scales and her elytra have 4 black ridges. **BIOLOGY:** Feeds on various daisy flowers. One of >1,000 spp. of monkey beetles known from South Africa, most of which are endemic to the region. **HABITAT:** Fynbos.

### African black beetle *Heteronychus arator*

**length 12–15mm** Shiny, black, with shallow longitudinal grooves on the elytra, each set with a series of distinct puncture marks. Front legs toothed for digging. **BIOLOGY:** Adults chew on the stems of plants just below ground level and bore into potato tubers. Larvae are C-shaped with red heads and feed underground on decomposing plant material. A serious introduced pest of lawns and crops in Australia and New Zealand. **HABITAT:** Grassland and farmland.

### Rhinoceros beetle *Oryctes boas*

**length 44mm** Large, well-known beetle, easily recognized by the long, backward-curving horn on the head of the male; head also has an anterior depression, edged by a ridge that extends into 2 small points dorsally. **BIOLOGY:** Large, C-shaped larvae feed on compost and manure. Adults burrow into young shoots of coconut palms and feed on the juices exuded. Nocturnal and often attracted to lights. **HABITAT:** Diverse habitats, especially savanna.

### Green dung beetle *Garreta nitens*

**length 13–18mm** Medium-sized, with a strongly domed pronotum; finely grooved elytra have a lateral indentation. Bright metallic green to coppery. **BIOLOGY:** Active by day. Male cuts a ball from fresh dung, rolls it away and buries it. Female later remodels the ball, laying a single egg within. When mature, larva pupates within the dung ball. One of several similar, metallic-coloured dung beetles. **HABITAT:** Savanna and bushveld, mainly in open woodland.

### Bronze dung beetle *Onitis alexis*

**length 16mm** Distinctive; bicoloured. Head and pronotum metallic green, elytra brown, longitudinally grooved and finely punctured with dots. **BIOLOGY:** Active morning and evening, digging tunnels beneath a dung pile and packing dung into sausage-shaped masses, into which eggs are laid. Mature larvae fashion pupal cases from their own faeces. Introduced into northern Australia to clear cattle dung and thus control flies. **HABITAT:** Diverse.

### Three-horned dung beetle
*Catharsius tricornutus*

**length 26mm** Large and black; male with a straight horn on the head and 2 diverging horns on the pronotum; elytra shiny black, lightly grooved. **BIOLOGY:** Nocturnal, burrows below or alongside fresh dung, packing dung into chambers at the ends of tunnels to make brood balls, each with a single egg. One of several horned species, some of which guard their broods. **HABITAT:** Mostly savanna and grassland.

### Flattened giant dung beetle
*Pachylomera femoralis*

**length 36–56mm** Massive, broad, flattened, dull black beetle with pronotum wider than the abdomen. Laterally curved forelegs powerfully developed, with front edges sculptured into large teeth. **BIOLOGY:** Active by day, often seen flying noisily toward fresh dung piles. Both sexes roll away dung for burial as brood balls and bury material in tunnels. **HABITAT:** Savanna and bushveld.

### Spider dung beetles
*Sisyphys* spp.

**length 3–12mm** Genus of small, grey to black dung beetles readily recognized by their extremely long hindlegs. **BIOLOGY:** Congregate to feed on fresh dung, especially that of small mammals. They roll away and bury dung, sometimes accepting the already formed oval dung pellets of antelope. The female lays a single egg in each ball. Some species leave their brood balls on the soil surface. **HABITAT:** Savanna, bushveld and forest.

### Water pennies
Family Psephenidae

**length 3mm** Small group with 4 spp. in SA; adults rarely seen, tiny, black, terrestrial, with soft elytra. Family best known, and named for, the flat, oval, aquatic larvae, which resemble limpets (shown, length 5mm). **BIOLOGY:** Females crawl under water to lay eggs, then die. Larvae scrape algae from rock surfaces using specialized limbs; their presence indicates good water quality. **HABITAT:** Larvae under rocks in fast streams, adults on nearby rocks and vegetation.

## Brush jewel beetles  *Julodis* spp.

**length 10–15mm** Large genus with 26 spp. in SA; highly spectacular, but variable and easily confused; patterned with tufts of wax-coated yellow, white or red hairs. **BIOLOGY:** Adults are short-lived and feed on foliage and flowers. Larvae dig into soil to feed on roots and are covered with large bristles pointing obliquely backward. **HABITAT:** Flowers and shrubs.

## Glittering jewel beetle
*Acmaeodera viridaenea*

**length 13mm** Smallish and common jewel beetle; head and pronotum strongly punctured, elytra with longitudinal ridges and rows of strong puncture marks. Male greenish brown with coppery sides, female metallic green to purple. Elytra fused together. **BIOLOGY:** Active in the middle of the day, feeding on flowers, especially those of *Acacia* spp. **HABITAT:** Flowers and vegetation.

## Giant jewel beetle  *Sternocera orissa*

**length 37mm** Large and distinctive; body greenish black, covered with yellow puncture marks; has large yellow spots on the sides of the pronotum and across the front and sides of the elytra. **BIOLOGY:** Adults fly clumsily, found mostly around *Acacia* flowers. Females drop large eggs onto soil and the larvae feed on roots. **HABITAT:** Savanna, bushveld and forest.

## Click beetles  Family Elateridae

**length 4–80mm** Very diverse, with ± 700 spp. in SA; small to very large, elongate, parallel-sided. Hind corners of the large pronotum form characteristic points. Brown or black, but some with white, yellow or orange spots. *Tetralobus flabellicornis* (length 60–80mm) shown. **BIOLOGY:** Click beetles leap into the air with a loud click when stranded on their backs, using a spine-and-notch mechanism on the underside. Adults feed nocturnally on foliage; larvae ('wireworms') are long and cylindrical, feeding underground on roots and tubers. **HABITAT:** Bushveld, forest and grassland.

### Fireflies and glowworms  Family Lampyridae

**length 6–25mm**  Soft-bodied, parallel-sided, mostly black or brown; males (left-hand image) with large eyes. *Luciola* sp. (length 7mm) shown. **BIOLOGY:** Family known for organs on lower abdomen that flash light to attract mates. In fireflies both sexes winged; in glowworms only males are winged, females (right-hand image) look like larvae. Larvae prey on slugs and snails. Adults are predatory, feed on pollen or do not feed. **HABITAT:** Woodland and moist grassland.

### Net-winged beetles  Family Lycidae

**length 6–25mm**  ± 50 spp. in SA; flattened, soft-bodied, often brightly coloured in brick red and black. Antenna long and serrated, elytra often laterally expanded and marked with longitudinal and transverse ridges (hence common name). *Lycus trabeatus* (length 18–22mm) shown. **BIOLOGY:** Lycidae contain a compound distasteful to predators. They feed by day on nectar from various plants. Larvae live in decaying wood or leaf litter. **HABITAT:** Forest, savanna and grassland.

### Hide beetles  Family Dermestidae

**length 2–10mm**  ± 30 spp. in SA; smallish, oval, with clubbed antennae that fit into grooves. Body usually covered with white or coloured scales. *Dermestes maculatus* (length 8mm) shown. **BIOLOGY:** Dermestidae feed on pollen and nectar, but the hairy brown larvae eat decaying animal matter; used to estimate time of death. May damage wool, other natural fibres, even museum specimens. Sometimes used to clean flesh from skeletons. **HABITAT:** Diverse.

### Auger borers  Family Bostrichidae

**length 2–32mm**  ± 60 spp. in SA; cylindrical, dark brown to black, most with a characteristic squared-off rear. Head points downward and is hidden by pronotum; antennae clubbed. *Apate femoralis* (length 12mm) shown. **BIOLOGY:** Auger borers and their fat white larvae are wood borers, attacking live trees and wood products, like furniture. Smaller species attack stored grain, dried fruit and cereal products. Includes significant introduced grain-boring pests. **HABITAT:** Wood.

## Chequered beetles         Family Cleridae

**length 2–30mm** Diverse, with ± 200 spp. in SA; elongate, parallel-sided, with large heads and hairy bodies, antennae serrate or clubbed. Black or with bright transverse bands; some, like *Gyponyx signifer* (shown, length 14mm), mimic velvet ants (p.133). **BIOLOGY:** Some chequered beetles are predatory, others feed on flowers or foliage. Larvae cylindrical, with 2 horn-like projections on the last segment; they usually feed on the larvae of wood-boring beetles. **HABITAT:** Diverse; larvae common in dead wood.

## Soft-winged flower beetles
Family Melyridae

**length 4–11mm** Diverse, with >250 spp. in SA; generally small, elongate and soft-bodied, often brightly coloured, some covered with erect hairs. **BIOLOGY:** Adults are predators or pollen-feeders, larvae are mostly carnivorous. Spotted maize beetle *Astylus atromaculatus* (shown, length 10mm), introduced from South America, is strikingly patterned and a minor pest of maize and other crops. Toxic to livestock. **HABITAT:** Mainly flowers.

## Ship-timber beetles         Family Lymexylidae

**length 15–45mm** Small and rarely encountered family with only 3 spp. in SA; easily recognized, very elongate and narrow, quite large brown beetles. Elytra short, exposing the abdomen and sometimes most of the folded hindwings. *Atractocerus brevicornis* (length 29mm) shown. **BIOLOGY:** Ship-timber beetle larvae are cylindrical and bore into wood, eating fungi that they culture in their tunnels. Some are significant pests of trees and timber. May be attracted to lights. **HABITAT:** Adults found in decaying wood or under bark.

## Ladybird beetles
Family Coccinellidae

**length 1–10mm** Diverse, with >200 spp. in SA; easily recognizable, smallish and hemispherical, with head sunken into the thorax, legs short, and elytra often brightly spotted or striped. Larvae and adults usually carnivorous, but some are herbivorous.

### Black-ringed ladybird
*Oenopia cinctella*

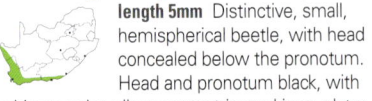

**length 5mm** Distinctive, small, hemispherical beetle, with head concealed below the pronotum. Head and pronotum black, with white to pale yellow geometric markings, elytra orange-yellow with black borders. **BIOLOGY:** Both adults and the tapering, yellow-and-black larvae are active predators on small insects and are used in biological pest control. **HABITAT:** Plant stems.

### Spotted amber ladybird
*Hippodamia variegata*

**length 4mm** Small, glossy hemispherical, with black and pale yellow head and pronotum. Elytra bright red with yellow anterior patch and, usually, 9, but up to 13, black dots. **BIOLOGY:** The adults and spiky black-and-orange larvae prey on aphids; widely used for pest control. A beneficial species introduced from Europe. **HABITAT:** Stems and leaves.

### Lunate ladybird
*Cheilomenes lunata*

**length 7mm** Distinctive, glossy, hemispherical beetle with black-and-yellow head and pronotum, and elytra distinctively patterned with large red spots on a black background. Larvae active, spiky, with black-and-yellow patterns. **BIOLOGY:** Adults and larvae prey on aphids; common on aphid-infested plants. **HABITAT:** Plant stems, especially sow thistles, *Sonchus* spp.

### Herbivorous ladybirds
*Epilachna* spp.

**length 6–8mm** Medium-sized, hemispherical beetles with elytra variously patterned in red and black and covered with short whitish down. Larvae covered with long, spiny projections. *Epilachna dregei* (length 8mm) shown. **BIOLOGY:** *Epilachna* adults and larvae are herbivorous, damaging leaves so that only a network of veins remains. Several species are pests of potatoes, tomatoes and cucumbers. **HABITAT:** Food plants.

## Darkling beetles
Family Tenebrionidae

**length 5–55mm** Extremely diverse, with thousands of species in SA. Medium-sized to very large, predominantly black beetles, mostly smooth, but some are strongly sculptured. Most live on the ground, the majority feeding on fresh or decaying plant matter. Some are significant pests of stored food products. Many are abundant in hot, dry regions, such as the Namib, where a few have evolved the unusual habit of standing head-down on the dunes, so that fog condenses on their elytra and runs down to the mouth, where it is swallowed.

### Frantic tortoise beetle
*Zophosis testudinaria*

**length 14mm** Flattened, smoothly oval black beetle with long antennae and long, slender legs. Develops a pinkish waxy bloom under hot, dry conditions. Elytra with small, flattened tubercles. **BIOLOGY:** Adults active in the heat of the day. Feed on plant and animal detritus, as well as on subterranean plant stems. **HABITAT:** Dry areas, where they scuttle about on coarse sand.

### Striped toktokkie
*Psammodes striatus*

**length 24mm** Familiar, large, globular beetle. Black with longitudinal red lines on the elytra. Male has pale yellow felt patch under the abdomen. **BIOLOGY:** Known for their habit of communicating with one another by tapping the abdomen repeatedly on the ground, in sequences of 4–20 taps at a time. Similar white-legged, plain black species are common in the northern parts of SA. **HABITAT:** Ground-dwelling (flightless).

### Spindle toktokkie
*Phanerotoma bertolonii*

**length 53mm** Very large, unusually elongated toktokkie beetle with tapering, ridged elytra and distinctive yellowish downy stripe along the sides of the body. **BIOLOGY:** Flightless, ground-dwelling species. Like others in the group, adults tap on the ground with the abdomen to locate and attract mates. Feeds on plant and animal material. **HABITAT:** Woodland and forest.

### Long-legged ground beetles  *Stenocara* spp.

**length 14–20mm** Medium-sized black beetles with unusually long, spindly legs. Several species are common; in some the elytra are ornamented with longitudinal ridges, in others with longitudinal rows of tubercles. Some develop a white waxy bloom on the body. **BIOLOGY:** Scavenge for plant and animal material and known for their habit of standing head-down in morning mist to collect drops of water, which condense on the body and run down to the mouth. **HABITAT:** Arid regions.

### Streaked ground beetle  *Cryptochile assimilis*

**length 12mm** Smallish brown beetle with stout, creamy-white legs; elytra have longitudinal ridges and are streaked and spotted with an attractive pattern of buff spots. Antennae dark brown. Body covered with tiny scales. **BIOLOGY:** Adults active in spring and scavenge for plant and animal material in drier coastal regions. **HABITAT:** Succulent and Nama karoo.

### Dusty maize beetle  *Gonocephalum simplex*

**length 10mm** Smallish, parallel-sided, flattened brownish beetle covered with flat, scale-like hairs. Pronotum extends forward distinctively on either side of the head. Elytra with low longitudinal ridges. **BIOLOGY:** A common pest of many crops, including coffee, rice, grapes and maize. Adults ringbark stems or feed on leaves or growing tips. Larvae feed on, and destroy, germinating seeds, especially those of cereals. **HABITAT:** Diverse; common in gardens.

## Metallic tree darkling beetle
*Strongylium purpuripenne*

**length 26mm** Unlike most darkling beetles, it is brightly coloured and not found on the ground. Head, pronotum and legs bright metallic green. Elytra bright metallic copper, with longitudinal ridges ornamented with distinct puncture marks. Royal tree darkling beetle *Metallonotus aerugineus* has similar appearance, habits and distribution, but head and pronotum are coppery and elytra are purple and lack ridges. **BIOGRAPHY:** Not known, probably feeds on dead plant material. **HABITAT:** Tree trunks in subtropical forest.

## Yellow mealworm
*Tenebrio molitor*

**length 15mm** Adult dark brown to black, with rectangular pronotum and elongate elytra with punctured longitudinal grooves. **BIOLOGY:** Known for its long-lived, cylindrical, yellowish larvae that are cultured in laboratories and pet shops as food for carnivorous animals, or to clean skeletons. Also grown as human food. Adults and larvae feed on a wide variety of plant and animal material, especially grains. **HABITAT:** Usually found in stored food products.

## Ant beetles
Family Anthicidae

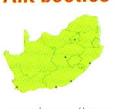

**length 2–9mm** ± 100 spp. in SA; small, usually black or metallic blue, with smooth, not grooved, elytra; body in 3 clear sections (head, pronotum and abdomen); legs slender. Shaped like an ant, hence 'ant beetles'. *Formicomus caeruleus* (length 4mm) shown. **BIOLOGY:** Adults eat plant and animal material; many are attracted to blister beetle larvae; may be useful for biological control. Larvae eat insect eggs or scavenge. **HABITAT:** Rotting plant or animal material; vegetation.

### Tumbling flower beetles
Family Mordellidae

**length 2–10mm** ± 36 spp. in SA; small, humpbacked beetles; head bends down and abdomen tapers to a point that extends well beyond elytra. Hindlegs longer than first 2 pairs and have swollen bases. Usually brown or black. **BIOLOGY:** Exhibit characteristic tumbling escape reaction when disturbed. **HABITAT:** Adults usually in flowers, especially daisies. Larvae in decaying wood or bore into stems.

### Blister beetles
Family Meloidae

**length–40mm** Diverse, ± 350 spp. in SA. Soft, elongate beetles with a large head separated from the narrow pronotum by a distinct neck. Well known for secreting the strong blistering agent cantharidin and frequently marked with bright warning colours. Adults feed on flowers, foliage or nectar; larvae parasitize or prey on bees or grasshopper eggs.

### Red-banded blister beetle
*Actenodia curtula*

**length 11mm** Smallish, black, covered with erect hairs, elytra each marked with 3 inner and 3 outer red spots, which may merge into transverse bands. **BIOLOGY:** Feeds on flowers. Like other blister beetles secretes the toxin cantharidin, which causes blistering of the skin. Bright coloration serves as a warning to potential predators. **HABITAT:** Flowers.

### CMR beetle
*Mylabris oculata*

**length 27mm** Large, conspicuous; head and pronotum black, elytra black with 2 broad yellow bands. Name refers to the colours of the old Cape Mounted Rifles corps. **BIOLOGY:** Can be a serious pest of ornamental, fruit and vegetable crops. Adults secrete cantharidin. Larvae parasitize grasshoppers' egg pods. One of several similarly coloured species. **HABITAT:** Flowers.

### Oil beetle
*Meloe angulatus*

**length 26mm** Large, shiny, flightless, bluish black, with narrow, sculptured head and pronotum, very short elytra and no hindwings. **BIOLOGY:** Name refers to cantharidin-containing 'blood' secreted from the joints when disturbed. Larvae grasp bees and are carried to the hive, where they feed on bee eggs, nectar and pollen. **HABITAT:** Low vegetation or on the ground.

## Carpenter bee blister beetle
*Synhoria testacea*

**length 22–35mm** Large, distinctive, 'sealing-wax red' beetle with black legs and antennae. Male has huge mandibles; their function is unknown, as adults are thought not to feed. **BIOLOGY:** The first instar larvae hitch rides on carpenter bees of the genus *Xylocopa* (p.137) and parasitize their nests and broods. **HABITAT:** Patchily distributed, usually close to logs with carpenter bees' nests.

## Longhorn beetles
Family Cerambycidae

**length 3–100mm** Large and diverse family, with >650 spp. in SA; medium-sized to very large, elongate, usually cylindrical beetles. The extremely long antennae, often held swept back along the body when at rest, are characteristic. Nocturnal and ground-dwelling species are often cryptic, while diurnal ones are usually brightly coloured. Larvae burrow into wood and some are serious pests of timber or living trees, their presence often revealed by piles of wood shavings ('frass') ejected from tunnel entrances. Adults feed on pollen, nectar, leaves or wood.

## Pondo-pondo longhorn
*Ceroplesis thunbergii*

**length 24mm** Body heavily textured with puncture marks and strikingly marked with 3 sets of alternating red and black transverse bands. Head, antennae and legs black. **BIOLOGY:** Eggs laid in slits in the bark of wattle trees, *Acacia* spp., into which the larvae burrow. Adults feed on bark. One of several similarly coloured species. *C. capensis* has similar habits, but has 4, not 3, sets of black and red bands. **HABITAT:** Trees.

## Eucalyptus borers
*Phoracantha* spp.

**length 25mm** Yellowish brown, with a distinctive pattern on the elytra comprising either 2 black spots (in *P. recurva*) or a zigzagging band (as in *P. semipunctata* shown here), followed by a broad black band. **BIOLOGY:** Accidentally introduced from Australia to many regions of the world, possibly along with railway sleepers. Adults are nocturnal, fly strongly and disperse widely. The larvae are economically significant pests of cultivated eucalyptus, burrowing deep into the wood, killing trees and damaging timber. **HABITAT:** Eucalyptus trees.

### Common metallic longhorn
*Promeces longipes*

**length 14mm** Medium-sized, narrow and elongate beetle. Body, legs and antennae are a vivid, metallic green-blue. **BIOLOGY:** Larvae bore into the stems of *Rhus* trees. Adults usually found on flowers and are conspicuous in flight. One of several similar metallic-looking species found in this and related genera. The Large green longhorn *Philematium natalense* is larger (length 25mm) and wider, with black antennae and red bases to the legs. **HABITAT:** Flowers in forest and bush.

### Giant longhorn
*Tithoes confinis*

**length 60–90mm** Massive, dark brown, with impressive, toothed jaws and 2 spikes on either side of the pronotum. Body covered with pale hairs that rub off, leaving dark brown patches. **BIOLOGY:** Adults nocturnal; may be attracted to lights. Larvae bore into trees in the mango family (Anacardiaceae), including cashew nut. One of the largest beetles in the region. **HABITAT:** Tree trunks.

### Leaf beetles
Family Chrysomelidae

**length 1–35 mm** Diverse and frequently encountered family including well over 1,000 spp. in SA; small to medium-sized beetles of variable shape. Most are glossy and conspicuously coloured in reds and yellows, some resemble ladybirds (but have 4, not 3, visible tarsal segments), while others are elongate. Both larvae and adults are herbivorous and some are serious pests of cultivated plants.

### Tobacco slug
*Lema daturaphila*

**length 7mm** Pronotum orange with 2 black spots, elytra pale yellow with longitudinal rows of puncture marks and 3 black longitudinal stripes. **BIOLOGY:** A well-known pest introduced from South America. Adults and larvae feed on Cape gooseberry and tobacco plants, feeding beneath the leaves. Larvae are camouflaged by piles of excrement carried on their backs. Previously known as *Lema trilineata*. **HABITAT:** Mostly in gardens.

## Flea beetles
*Blepharida* spp.

**length 6mm** Head and pronotum brown with small cream markings, elytra punctured and marked with tile-like brown and cream patches. **BIOLOGY:** Hindlegs strongly developed for jumping. Larvae caterpillar-like, with a sucking disc at the posterior end, and may retain faeces on their backs for camouflage. Adults jump vigorously if disturbed. Related species feed on poisonous plants; the San traditionally squeezed the poisonous body fluids of *Blepharida* larvae onto their arrowheads. **HABITAT:** Host plants.

## Dune tortoise beetle
*Aspidomorpha puncticosta*

**length 13mm** Broad, flattened beetle with head hidden under the transparent pronotum; elytra largely transparent, with 5 black patches around the border and fine white veins. **BIOLOGY:** Larvae (bottom image) are spiky and retain the moults of earlier larval instars on the end of the abdomen, which is held curled over the body. Feed on the Dune morning glory *Ipomoea pescaprae*. **HABITAT:** Coastal dunes adjacent to beaches.

## Spotted tortoise beetle
*Conchyloctenia punctata*

**length 11mm** Moderately flattened, oval beetle with head hidden under the orange pronotum; elytra gold to red, with black dots. **BIOLOGY:** Eggs laid in a papery brownish egg case attached to the leaves of morning glory plants, *Ipomoea* spp. Larvae flattened, oval, pink-and-black spotted and spiny, often retaining the moults of earlier instars on their backs. This species often co-occurs with the more flattened, bright golden Fool's gold beetle *Aspidomorpha tecta*. **HABITAT:** Morning glory plants.

### Pea (bean) weevils
Subfamily Bruchidae

**length 2–5mm** Small, compact and oval; generally black, brown or mottled, usually with grooved elytra. **BIOLOGY:** Adults deposit eggs on seeds, into which the larvae burrow to feed. Larvae cut a distinctive exit hole before pupating. Adults feign death and drop from plants when disturbed. Several species are pests, but *Neltumius arizonensis* (shown, length 4mm) was deliberately imported into South Africa as a biocontrol agent for mesquite trees, *Prosopis* spp. **HABITAT:** Pea weevils occur on vegetation, especially legumes.

### Fungus weevils
Family Anthribidae

**length 3–30mm** Oblong, usually dark beetles, often patterned with scales or hairs. One-spot fungus weevil *Chirotenon longimanus* (shown, length 21mm) has a short, broad snout, a mottled body with a distinct cream posterior patch and distinctive, elongate, black-and-white striped legs. **BIOLOGY:** Most adults feed on fungi or decaying matter; the larvae feed on dead wood. **HABITAT:** Subtropical forest.

### Primitive weevils
Family Brentidae

**length 4–20mm** Variable in shape, but usually elongate, parallel-sided, with non-elbowed antennae, swollen legs and more-or-less elongate snout. The Cycad weevil *Antliarhinus zamiae* (shown, length 9mm) has an extraordinarily long, thin snout with mandibles at the tip. **BIOLOGY:** Female of *A. zamiae* uses the mandibles to drill into the scales of cycad cones to reach the seeds, within which she lays eggs. Larvae feed on, and pupate inside, the seeds. **HABITAT:** Associated with cycads.

## Common weevils
Family Curculionidae

**length 2–60mm** One of the largest insect families, with >2,500 spp. in SA, showing enormous variety; all with a long snout ending in mandibles; elbowed and clubbed antennae are attached to the side of the snout. Adults and larvae are herbivorous.

### Prong-tailed weevil
*Hipporrhinus furvus*

**length 30mm** Large, elongated, heavily built weevil with thick, curved snout and elbowed antennae that end in clubs. Entire body covered with pronounced black knobs, with whitish or pinkish scales between them; elytra end in 2 prongs. **BIOLOGY:** Flightless and easily recognized; little known of its habits. **HABITAT:** Ground-dwelling in diverse habitats.

### Snout weevils
*Sciobius* spp.

**length 10mm** Endemic genus of ± 50 spp. of medium-sized, flightless weevils recognized by a V-shaped notch at the tip of the rostrum, as viewed from above. Antennae long and elbowed. Colour highly variable: some being dull brown with buff hairs, others iridescent blue. **BIOLOGY:** Larvae feed on roots; some are pests of citrus and potatoes. **HABITAT:** Adults found in the foliage of litchi and other trees.

### Red-spotted lily weevil
*Brachycerus ornatus*

**length 25–45mm** Spectacular, large, ground-dwelling weevil. Head strongly ridged, pronotum with rounded tubercles, abdomen rounded. Body and legs black, body with red spots and markings. **BIOLOGY:** Feeds on Karoo lily, *Ammocharis coranica*. Female lays eggs in burrows adjacent to lily bulbs, on which larvae feed before pupating in the soil. **HABITAT:** Ground-dwelling; associated with Karoo lilies.

### Maize (rice) weevil
*Sitophilus oryzae*

**length 2–5mm** Tiny, dark brown, winged, with 4 reddish patches on the elytra. Body with closely spaced rows of punctures and long, thick snout. **BIOLOGY:** Female uses strong mandibles to chew a hole in a grain kernel, laying a single egg within it and sealing the hole. Larva feeds within the grain, hollowing it out. A serious pest of stored wheat, rice and maize. **HABITAT:** Grain-storage areas and agricultural fields.

# TWISTED WING PARASITES
**Order Strepsiptera**

A small order; South African fauna includes only ± 12 spp. Larvae mostly internal parasites of insect hosts, but the most primitive members are free-living parasites of fish moths. Pupae protrude from abdominal segments of the host; winged males exit the pupal skin and take to the air on large, fan-shaped hindwings. Rudimentary forewings used as balancing organs during flight. Males use their antler-shaped antennae, and bulging compound eyes, to locate females, which remain in their pupal skins, are wingless and legless, and have a fused head and thorax. After mating, females release large numbers of mobile 'triangulin' larvae, which seek out new hosts.

### Twisted wing parasites
*Family Stylopidae*

**length 4mm** Largest and most widespread family with 10 spp. in SA. In males (*Xenos* shown, length 4mm) the last 2 segments of the antennae form large, flat plates that are held parallel. **BIOLOGY:** Species shown parasitizes *Ammophila* wasps (p.135). **HABITAT:** Small, cryptic and seldom observed; the most common hosts are bees and wasps of the families Vespidae (p.134) and Sphecidae (p.135).

# HANGINGFLIES AND SCORPION FLIES
**Order Mecoptera**

A small order of slender, predatory insects with a single family and 31 spp. in SA. Adults have 2 pairs of equal-sized, clear brown wings, and long, strong legs, ending in long, powerful tarsi used to subdue prey. Males give captured prey to females during courtship. The mouthparts form a tube (the 'rostrum') with sharp, serrated mandibles for cutting through the exoskeleton of prey. The larvae are predaceous and resemble caterpillars, but have 8, not 5, pairs of false legs under the abdomen.

## Hangingflies
*Family Bittacidae*

**wingspan 40–60mm** Body slender, but limbs long and powerful, with long tarsi to hold prey. Wings narrow, membranous, folded together at rest. Use serrated mandibles to cut into prey, then inject salivary enzymes and drain the body.

### Hangingflies
*Bittacus* spp.

**wingspan 40mm** Body orange, with clear brown wings of equal size. Posture diagnostic: usually hang from vegetation by 1 or 2 front legs. Antennae long and thread-like. Tarsi black and raptorial. **BIOLOGY:** Can subdue large prey. Females choose males that present largest prey gifts during courtship. Attracted to lights. Adults present only for a brief period every year. **HABITAT:** Moist grassland and forest edges.

# FLIES
## Order Diptera

A very large order with ± 16,000 spp. in the Afrotropics. Adults have a single pair of wings on the middle thoracic segment (the 'mesothorax'), and a pair of reduced, drumstick-shaped hindwings on the last thoracic segment (the 'metathorax'), used for balancing during flight. The mouthparts are usually modified for sucking up fluid, not for biting: they sometimes form an extensible sucking pad or long, tubular proboscis. Ecology of the group is diverse, although primitive groups are typically associated with water, especially as larvae. Larvae highly varied in form and habits. Many blood-feeding species are key vectors of diseases such as malaria.

### Craneflies         Family Tipulidae

**length 10–25mm** Large family; ± 250 spp. in SA; medium-sized to large, with very long, thin legs, long antennae, a V-shaped groove on the thorax and tube-like mouthparts. *Nephrotoma* sp. (wingspan 28mm) shown has shiny black-and-yellow body; common in gardens. **BIOLOGY:** Larvae ('leatherjackets') feed on grass roots; adults do not feed. **HABITAT:** Larvae live in streambeds, moist litter, compost and soil. Adults common in wet, dank areas, like forests and vleis.

### Mothflies         Family Psychodidae

**length up to 6mm** ± 30 spp. in SA; small and moth-like. Mottled grey wings broad and triangular, covered with hairs and held open and flat over the body. Larvae cylindrical, light black and hairy. *Clogmia albipunctata* (shown, wingspan 6mm) is cosmopolitan; always found in association with human habitation. **BIOLOGY:** Larvae feed on fungal mats and are important for the free draining of trickle filters used on sewerage farms. **HABITAT:** Adults sedentary; found on bathroom walls and near drains.

### Net-winged midges         Family Blephariceridae

**wingspan 12mm** One regional genus *Elporia* (shown, wingspan 12mm) with 19 spp. in SA; small black flies with creases in the wings as a result of folding in the pupa. Legs long and spindly. Unusual larvae with 5–6 constricted body segments, each with a large ventral sucker. **BIOLOGY:** Adults fly just above water surface. **HABITAT:** Fast-flowing mountain streams; adults often aggregate at the sides of midstream rocks; larvae found under rocks.

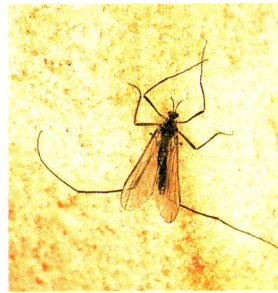

### Midges, gnats and bloodworms
Family Chironomidae

**wingspan 3–14mm** Diverse group with >175 spp. in SA; small, mosquito-like; body grey, green or yellow, thorax humped. Males have very fluffy antennae. Forelegs are longer than the other legs (*Chironomus formosipennis* shown, wingspan 12mm). Larvae diverse, but generally C-shaped and often bright red. **BIOLOGY:** Adults short-lived, often attracted to lights in large numbers. Larvae feed on detritus. **HABITAT:** The larvae are aquatic; ubiquitous in most water bodies. Red larvae of *Chironomus* typical of anaerobic muds at the bottom of ponds. Adults especially abundant near water, where they may form mating swarms.

## Mosquitoes
Family Culicidae

**wingspan 6–18mm** Includes ± 133 spp. in SA. Lightly built, familiar insects, hindlegs usually held up in the air at rest. Blood-feeding females are significant vectors of malaria and other diseases, such as yellow fever, elephantiasis, dengue fever and encephalitis. Males feed on nectar and do not bite. Both sexes beat their wings rapidly, producing a characteristic whine in flight. Larvae have a distinct head capsule and are generally found in enriched water bodies, breathing via a short siphon at the end of the abdomen.

### Bush mosquitoes
*Aedes* spp.

**wingspan 6–8mm** Black-and-white banded legs, wings smoky black. **BIOLOGY:** They bite during the day, transmitting yellow fever and elephantiasis in certain areas. **HABITAT:** Larvae breed in water collected in the axils of plants, such as those of the Natal wild banana *Strelitzia nicolai*; adults are common in indigenous forests, but may also occur indoors.

### House mosquitoes
*Culex* spp.

**wingspan 8mm** Small, dull brown, with a yellow-striped abdomen. Probably the most common mosquitos found in domestic settings and that bite humans. **BIOLOGY:** They breed in small containers of water, such as buckets and gutters. In certain areas adults transmit elephantiasis. **HABITAT:** Ubiquitous and abundant in urban settings.

### Biting midges  Family Ceratopogonidae

**length 3mm** ± 130 spp. in SA; very small, short-legged, dark, with clear wings folded neatly over the back at rest. **BIOLOGY:** Adults feed on the blood of vertebrates, including that of humans. The painless bite is followed by intense itching that can last for weeks. Adults may transmit bluetongue disease to sheep and African horse sickness to equids. A few feed off the 'blood' from the veins in insect wings. **HABITAT:** Larvae develop in moist soil and vleis; adults common in most areas, and in spring in the winter-rainfall region.

### Blackflies  Family Simuliidae

**wingspan 5–6mm** ± 44 spp. in SA; small, stocky, dark brown, with a humped thorax and short legs, wings rounded and sometimes opaque. Aquatic larvae (bottom image) are elongated and dark, with a pair of fans on the head capsule for filter feeding. **BIOLOGY:** Females well known for their blood-sucking habit, feeding from vertebrates, including humans; may transmit the parasite for elephantiasis and river blindness. Form large swarms along the Orange River, where they pester cattle. **HABITAT:** Larvae congregate on rocks in the fastest-flowing parts of rivers; adults are most common fairly near to large rivers and streams.

### March flies  Family Bibionidae

**wingspan 8–12mm** 18 spp. in SA; small black-and-orange flies with black wings and very large eyes. Legs long and spindly. *Plecia ruficollis* shown (wingspan 12mm). Genus *Bibio* comprises smaller black species with swollen femora and includes most of the region's March flies. **BIOLOGY:** Adults are slow-moving; may form mating swarms in spring. Larvae are soil-dwelling, feeding on the underground parts of plants. **HABITAT:** Widespread, but absent from the very arid interior. Adults common on daisy flowers.

### Gall midges
Family Cecidomyiidae

**length up to 3mm** Diverse, but with only 25 spp. in SA; very small and spindly, with long, thin legs and antennae. Antennae bead-like, with a whorl of hairs arising at each segment. Wings large, rounded and fringed with hairs. **BIOLOGY:** Adults seldom seen, but galls containing the larvae are conspicuous on host plants (galls shown were formed by an Acacia gallfly *Dasineura dielsi*). Host plant and appearance of the galls are good identifying characteristics. **HABITAT:** Ubiquitous across the region. Some species are pests of millet, rice and sorghum crops.

### Soldier flies
Family Stratiomyiidae

**wingspan 16–25mm** 112 spp. in SA; medium-sized to large, with long wings neatly folded across the back, abdomen flat. Often brightly coloured and mimic wasps. *Hermetia illucens* (shown, wingspan 16mm) is a common, cosmopolitan species with a clear panel at the junction of the abdomen and thorax. Larvae (bottom image) hard and flattened, lacking appendages. **BIOLOGY:** Adults sluggish. *H. illucens* larvae are common and beneficial decomposers of garden compost and agricultural and abattoir waste, and are cultured as poultry feed. **HABITAT:** Common in moist areas, including gardens.

### Dark-winged fungus gnats
Family Sciaridae

**wingspan 7mm** 26 spp. in SA; thorax humped, legs stout and abdomen swollen. Eyes meet to form a bridge above the antennae. Body and wings often black. **BIOLOGY:** Larvae feed mostly on fungi, but also on plants and rotting wood. Adults occasionally feed on nectar. **HABITAT:** Most habitats, but especially common in moist forest and mesic grassland; often on the soil around indoor pot plants.

## Snipe flies
Family Rhagionidae

**length 10–18mm** 24 spp. in SA; slender, long-legged, with a prominent proboscis. Eyes large, abdomen often striped in black and yellow. The Wormlion fly *Leptynoma sericea* (shown, wingspan 16mm) has smoky brown wings. **BIOLOGY:** Wormlion larvae inhabit conical pits, like those of antlions (p.63), in fine sand in the rain shadows of rock overhangs and caves, where they trap small prey. Adults feed on flowers. Other snipe flies have aquatic larvae. **HABITAT:** Wormlions occur in the arid parts of the winter-rainfall region, as well as in cool forests in the summer-rainfall region.

## Water snipe flies
Family Athericidae

**wingspan 10–16mm** Small, primitive, with ± 16 spp. in SA; resemble small horseflies (Tabanidae, below) with smoky grey or brown wings and thin, stiletto-like mouthparts for taking blood meals. Female *Trichacantha atranupta* is brown; the larger, yellowish male (shown, wingspan 16mm) has greatly elongated, splayed hindlegs. **BIOLOGY:** Some feed on the blood of unusual hosts, such as owls and frogs. **HABITAT:** Associated with fast mountain streams in forests.

## Horseflies (clegs)
Family Tabanidae

Includes at least 230 spp. in SA; medium-sized to large flies with a sometimes greatly elongated, stabbing proboscis, large, iridescent eyes, and a V-shaped space between the veins at the wing tips. Adults feed on blood and nectar; larvae eat decomposing vegetable matter, aquatic insects and even tadpoles. Females spread the diseases surra and nagana in cattle and the parasitic loa loa worm, which lives around the eyeballs in humans.

## Green-eyed horseflies
*Rhigioglossa* spp.

**wingspan 20mm** Medium-sized, clear-winged horseflies with emerald-green wings and a short, stout proboscis. Body striped grey and orange. **BIOLOGY:** Common pests in spring in winter-rainfall areas, where the females settle silently onto mammals before giving a painful bite. Also feed on pollen and nectar and often heavily dusted with pollen. **HABITAT:** All vegetation types in the winter-rainfall region. Larvae occur in vleis and moist soil.

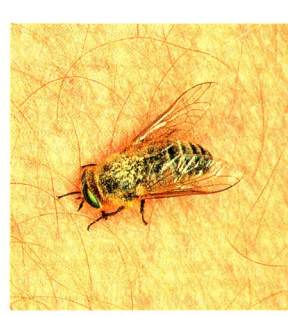

### Needle-nose fly
*Philoliche rostrata*

**wingspan 35–45mm** Large, grey, with black-and-grey/white striped abdomen, turning orange next to thorax. Proboscis very long, held out in front of the body. **BIOLOGY:** Adults feed on nectar of a range of plants, from pelargoniums to *Leucospermum* pincushions, and on the blood of mammals. Flies far and fast. **HABITAT:** Most vegetation types in the winter-rainfall region.

### Clegs
*Haematopota* spp.

**wingspan 22mm** Dark grey, with large, triangular, mottled grey wings and iridescent eyes. Many similar species in the region. **BIOLOGY:** Fly silently, often from shaded areas, to feed on mammal blood. Adults also take water from mud puddles. Larvae prey on other insects in moist soil. **HABITAT:** Occur in most parts of the region, but are rare in very arid areas.

### Mydas flies
Family Mydidae

**length 20mm** 195 spp. in SA; large, wasp-like, with conspicuous, clubbed antennae; abdomen banded, wings sometimes smoky and legs stout. *Afroleptomydas* sp. shown is a large (30mm wingspan) wasp mimic, with long mouthparts. **BIOLOGY:** Adults apparently feed on the nectar of ice plants (Aizoaceae). Larvae are soil-dwelling and feed on other insects. **HABITAT:** More common in the arid parts of the region, usually on bare ground with sparse vegetation cover or on rocks.

### Robber flies
Family Asilidae

**length 3–40mm** An important family, with >500 spp. in SA. Small to large, often bristly, flies that use their strong legs and stout, piercing mouthparts to subdue insect prey. Larvae are maggot-like and feed on rotting vegetable matter, other insects or locust egg pods.

### Bristly robber fly
*Dasypletis placodes*

**wingspan 19mm** Medium-sized, body covered with whitish-yellow bristles, eyes bright golden-green. Legs exceptionally bristly. In flight, resembles a sluggish bee. **BIOLOGY:** Feeds largely on bees and wasps (feeding on a mydas fly in this image). **HABITAT:** Sparse vegetation in bushveld and woodland.

### White-tufted robber flies   *Neolophonotus* spp.

**wingspan 16mm**  Medium-sized, dull grey; abdomen with black transverse markings above and a pair of white tufts on the underside. Thorax distinctly humped, eyes dull red. **BIOLOGY:** A common species. Tackles a range of insects, settling on open ground or rocks and making forays to intercept flying prey. **HABITAT:** Bare ground in arid succulent karoo vegetation and the barren interior.

### Tangle-veined flies   Family Nemestrinidae

**wingspan 25–50mm**  48 spp. in SA; large, conspicuous, with large wings and eyes and a very long proboscis. A number of veins run parallel along the wing tip. *Prosoeca* (wingspan 30mm) shown. **BIOLOGY:** Adults feed on various flowers, typically those with line markings in the throat. Many are the only pollinators of flowers with extremely long tubes. Larvae are internal parasites of other insects. **HABITAT:** Most common in succulent karoo and coastal fynbos.

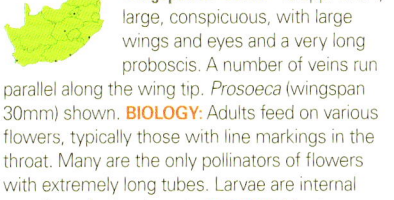

J. Manning

### Small-headed flies   Family Acroceridae

**wingspan 10–25mm**  ± 40 spp. in SA; unusual, medium-sized, with head hidden below humped thorax. Wings reinforced with fine folds; very long proboscis held between legs. *Psilodera fasciata* (shown, wingspan 22mm) has black-and-white striped abdomen and yellow legs. **BIOLOGY:** Adults eat nectar. Larvae internal parasites of spiders. **HABITAT:** Gardens and natural vegetation.

### Bee flies                                                       Family Bombyliidae

**length 4–40mm**  Very diverse family including ± 940 spp. in SA. Small to large, rotund, furry flies, often seen feeding on flowers. Most active at midday, they are often the only conspicuous insects seen during summer in the most arid parts of the region. Known for their very accurate hovering flight. Important pollinators.

### White-tipped bee fly   *Bombomyia discoidea*

**wingspan 20mm**  Conspicuous, large, with thorax black or orange and bases of wings black. Abdomen with white tip. **BIOLOGY:** Often seen taking nectar from daisy flowers, including thistles. Larvae parasitize solitary bees. **HABITAT:** Common and conspicuous throughout most of SA.

**FLIES**

### Golden bee fly
*Australoechus hirtus*

**wingspan 22mm** Very bee-like, evenly coated with long, golden-yellow hairs. Wings clear with light brown tinge, proboscis fairly long. **BIOLOGY:** Easily detected by the loud humming noise produced by the wings during flight and when hovering above the flowers of the ice plants (Aizoaceae) on which it feeds. Often basks on open sand. **HABITAT:** Areas with low, succulent vegetation; common on open ground.

### Dance flies
Family Empididae

**wingspan 10–15mm** Diverse family; ± 230 spp. in SA; small, grey, with long, stabbing proboscis, stout legs and small dent on inner edge of eyes. *Hilarempis* sp. (16mm wingspan) shown has grey body and grey (or black-and-yellow) legs. **BIOLOGY:** They buzz their wings to skate on top of the water surface, feeding on drowning insects. Males present females with a dead insect or empty silk ball before mating. **HABITAT:** On dams or vleis; also on the margins of streams.

### Long-legged flies
Family Dolichopodidae

**wingspan 7–18mm** 123 spp. in SA; small, bristly, with strong legs. Many are metallic golden-green, with dark markings on the wings, including *Condylostylus makalaka* (shown, wingspan 7mm). **BIOLOGY:** Adults perch on forest leaves and prey on smaller insects. **HABITAT:** Common on the upper surfaces of leaves, especially understorey plants in forests; rarer in arid parts.

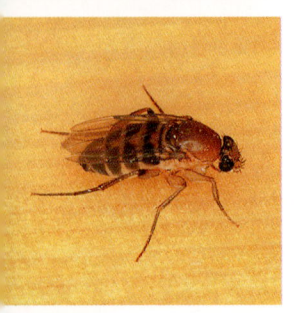

### Scuttle flies (coffin flies)
Family Phoridae

**wingspan 2–5mm** ± 58 spp. in SA; very small, with rapid, erratic, scuttling locomotion. Body black, brown or yellow, legs short and strong. The Common coffin fly *Megaselia scalaris* (shown, wingspan 4mm) is a small, cosmopolitan species, with yellow-and-black striped abdomen. **BIOLOGY:** Scuttle flies eat decaying animal matter. **HABITAT:** Ubiquitous and common in most habitats, including urban settings; may be trapped inside windows.

### Hover flies
Family Syrphidae

wingspan 6–20mm Important family, with 230 spp. in SA; common and conspicuous bee mimics; most species have a yellow-and-brown striped abdomen and very large eyes meeting in front of the head. A number of veins run parallel along the front margins of the wings. The Drone fly *Eristalis tenax* (shown, wingspan 15mm) is a small, stocky bee mimic; its unusual grey larvae ('rat-tailed maggots') have a very long breathing tube at the end of the abdomen. **BIOLOGY:** Adults excellent fliers, typically seen hovering precisely in sunlit glades or feeding on daisy flowers. The larvae of some species feed on aphids. **HABITAT:** Common in all vegetation types; some species abundant in gardens.

### Fruit beetle parasite flies
Family Pyrgotidae

wingspan 10–18mm 36 spp. in SA; medium-sized to large, brown, with a bulge at the front of the head. *Campylocera* sp. (shown, wingspan 14mm) is medium-sized, brown, with widely spaced eyes; female has long egg-laying tube ('ovipositor') projecting from the compressed abdomen. **BIOLOGY:** Active at dusk and at night; females locate scarab hosts on which to lay eggs while both are in flight. **HABITAT:** Forest and open woodland in warm, summer-rainfall areas.

### Big-headed flies
Family Conopidae

wingspan 10–18mm 65 spp. in SA; resemble small hover flies (Syrphidae, above), but have a narrow waist. Some species are convincing wasp mimics. Head enlarged. Body brown with yellow markings. *Conops zonatus* (shown) is a medium-sized brown fly (18mm wingspan) with conspicuous antennae and brown wings. **BIOLOGY:** Adults feed on nectar; larvae parasitize other insects, especially wasps. **HABITAT:** Rarely seen; they inhabit open woodland and bushveld.

### Fruit flies
Family Tephritidae

**wingspan 6–18mm** Diverse family; 375 spp. in SA; small to medium-sized, with conspicuously patterned wings and prominent, pointed ovipositor. The Natal fruit fly *Ceratitis rosa* (shown, wingspan 8mm) is stocky with iridescent eyes, broad wings marked with brown and brown-and-yellow stripes across the end of its thorax. **BIOLOGY:** Many, such as *C. rosa*, are significant agricultural pests. **HABITAT:** Ubiquitous, especially in grassland, forest and agricultural settings.

### Signal flies
Family Platystomatidae

**wingspan 15–50mm** ± 80 spp. in SA; medium-sized to large, sluggish and brightly coloured. *Bromophila caffra* (shown, wingspan 30–50mm) is a common, very large species with metallic black body and wings and a 'sealing-wax red' head. **BIOLOGY:** Both adults and larvae feed on decomposing animal and vegetable matter, as well as faecal waste. **HABITAT:** *B. caffra* adults often seen sitting in exposed positions on vegetation in warm, summer-rainfall areas.

### Bee lice
Family Braulidae

**length 1–1.5mm** Only 2 spp. in SA, both in genus *Braula*. Very small, wingless, oval flies with stout, grasping legs and with reduced antennae and eyes. **BIOLOGY:** External parasites of bees (see arrows). In the hive they scavenge food from workers feeding the queen. Larvae feed on wax combs and on pollen stored in wax cells. **HABITAT:** Found on free-flying drone bees and in beehives.

### Stilt-legged flies
Family Micropezidae

**wingspan 15–20mm** Only 4 spp. in SA; medium-sized, with very long, spindly, banded legs, the first pair shortest. *Mimegralla fuelleborni* (shown, wingspan 20mm) has a striped grey body and white tips to the forelegs. **BIOLOGY:** *M. fuelleborni* often occurs in groups; may mimic ichneumon wasps (p.130). Larvae probably feed on living or decaying plant matter, adults on rotting fruit. **HABITAT:** Stilt-legged flies found on understorey plants in forest and open woodland; also associated with rotting fruit in gardens.

### Banana stalk flies     Family Neriidae

**wingspan 8mm** Only 2 spp. in SA, both in genus *Chaetonerius*. Medium-sized, legs long and spindly, antennae with thin bristles and club-shaped bases; body with yellow and brown longitudinal stripes. **BIOLOGY:** Larvae feed on decaying plant matter, including ripe pumpkins. **HABITAT:** Forest and gardens, where adults rest head-downward on tree trunks or stand with an alert posture on ripe fruit.

### Stalk-eyed flies     Family Diopsidae

**wingspan 6–12mm** Some 33 spp. in SA; eyes at the end of medium-sized to long stalks; thorax bears a pair of spines; wings frequently marked with dark spots. *Diopsis* sp. (shown, wingspan 12mm) is small, with very long, thin eyestalks and orange head and abdomen. **BIOLOGY:** Adults slow-moving, aggregating at, and feeding on, plant exudates. Larvae bore into tender plant shoots. **HABITAT:** Common on rank grass and herbs, in forest, grassland and open woodland.

### Black scavenger flies     Family Sepsidae

**wingspan 4–6mm** 23 spp. in SA; small, common, black, brown or reddish, with a constricted abdomen and spherical head. In many species wing tips have a black spot. *Paratoxapoda* sp. (shown, wingspan 5mm) is a small, black fly with clear wings. **BIOLOGY:** Waves the wings about while feeding on dung or carcasses. **HABITAT:** Widespread, usually seen courting on larval substrate, like fresh dung, but most common in warm, summer-rainfall areas.

### Snail-killing flies     Family Sciomyzidae

**wingspan 10–16mm** 30 spp. in SA; medium-sized, yellow-brown; may have stripes running along length of thorax and spots on the wings. *Sepodon* sp. (shown, wingspan 12mm) is tan, with stout legs and brown-tinted wings. **BIOLOGY:** Snail-killing flies lay eggs on vegetation at water bodies; hatched larvae drop into the water. Larvae useful for biological control: they feed on aquatic snails, including those that transmit bilharzia. **HABITAT:** Stagnant or slow-flowing water bodies.

### Lauxaniid flies
Family Lauxaniidae

**wingspan 8–10mm** ± 42 spp. in SA; small, yellowish brown or black, with patterned wings and iridescent, bright red eyes. Resemble vinegar flies (p.101). *Cestrotus* sp. (wingspan 10mm) shown is recognized by heavily patterned wings, red eyes, stocky body and black-and-white band across head. **BIOLOGY:** Adults in small groups, feeding on flowers and fungi; larvae feed on leaf litter. **HABITAT:** *Cestrotus* spp. found on walls and river rocks.

### Kelp flies (seaweed flies)
Family Coelopidae

**wingspan 10–15mm** only 2 spp. in SA, both of genus *Coelopa* (shown, wingspan 16mm); resemble sluggish, hairy house flies (p.102), with strong, bristly legs. **BIOLOGY:** Associated with rotting beached kelp; adults and larvae both feed on kelp exudates and mucus. Adults may be blown inland in numbers, becoming a nuisance near coastal homes. **HABITAT:** Abundant on sandy and rocky shores with accumulations of beached kelp.

### Shore flies
Family Ephydridae

**wingspan 6–10mm** 70 spp. in SA; small to very small, grey or black, with hairy antennae; wings occasionally with pigmented spots. *Ochtera* sp. (wingspan 10mm) shown is among the largest members of the family; stocky, grey or bronze with enlarged forelegs for grasping prey. **BIOLOGY:** Adults abundant predators of small insects, larvae feed on various foods. **HABITAT:** Adults walk on algal mats at the edges of inland and estuarine water bodies.

### Sun flies
Family Heleomyzidae

**wingspan 10–15mm** ± 31 spp. in SA; medium-sized, wings are dark with lighter markings and seem to bend halfway along their length. *Suilla picta* (shown, wingspan 12mm) is mostly black, with broad, patterned wings, a small head and bright red eyes. **BIOLOGY:** Adults sluggish, perching on vegetation; larvae eat rotting plant and animal matter, including fungi, carrion and detritus in mammals' nests. **HABITAT:** Forest, open woodland and gardens.

### Cheese skippers — Family Piophilidae

**wingspan 4–6mm** Just 3 spp. in SA; small, shiny, bluish-black flies, with yellow legs and red eyes. The cosmopolitan Cheese skipper *Piophila casei* (wingspan 6mm) is shown. **BIOLOGY:** Adults and larvae feed on protein-rich foods such as cheese and dead animals, occasionally achieving pest status in homes and factories. **HABITAT:** Ubiquitous across the region, wherever suitable substrates occur.

### Dung flies — Family Scathophagidae

**length 3–11mm** Just 1 spp. in SA, *Scathophaga stercoraria* (shown, wingspan 16–20mm). Medium-sized, bristly, with small plates protecting the reduced second pair of wings (known as 'halteres'). Males larger, identified by dense yellow fur covering front legs. **BIOLOGY:** Adults feed on the nectar of various plants and mate on fresh dung, in which the larvae develop. **HABITAT:** Common near the coast on flowers, vegetation or dung in various vegetation types.

### Leaf-mining flies — Family Agromyzidae

**wingspan 4mm** Includes >130 spp. in SA; very small, elongated, black or yellow flies, sometimes with yellow markings on the thorax. *Liriomyza* sp. (wingspan 4mm) shown is yellow with a dark brown dorsal surface and a yellow spot between the wings; a significant pest species imported from North America. **BIOLOGY:** Larvae burrow ('mine') into leaves and young shoots of a variety of plants, including many vegetable crops. **HABITAT:** Western Cape sandveld, gardens and agricultural fields.

### Vinegar flies — Family Drosophiliidae

**wingspan 3–6mm** >60 spp. in SA; small, stocky, familiar flies, usually with bright red eyes. *Zaprionus* sp. (wingspan 4mm) shown has a pair of silver stripes running along the thorax. **BIOLOGY:** Vinegar fly adults hover above, and settle on, rotting fruit, attracted by the alcoholic odour released by fermenting yeasts. The small maggots feed on yeasts. **HABITAT:** Ubiquitous in all habitats, including gardens and houses.

### Jackal flies

Family Milichiidae
**wingspan 2–4mm** 13 spp. in SA; small, dark, grey-black flies, sometimes with red eyes. **BIOLOGY:** Most easily recognized by their habit of loitering around insect predators, such as spiders and assassin bugs (p.48), feeding on fluids escaping from the predated insect, as shown here. **HABITAT:** Ubiquitous, but usually seen in gardens in association with feeding crab spiders.

### Root-maggot flies

Family Anthomyiidae
**wingspan 10–15mm** ± 27 spp. in SA; resemble small grey house flies, although *Anthomyia* sp. (wingspan 10mm) shown has body with striking grey-and-black bands. **BIOLOGY:** Habits varied, larvae feeding on live and decaying plant matter. *Anthomyia* larvae have been reared from birds' nests. **HABITAT:** Ubiquitous. This family also includes the Kelp fly *Fucellia capensis*, found in association with kelp flies *Coelopa* spp. (p.100) on beached seaweed.

### House flies

Family Muscidae
**wingspan 9–15mm** Large family, with at least 364 spp. in SA; most commonly seen flies belong to this family, but can only be identified using microscopic features. The Common house fly *Musca domestica* (shown, wingspan 9–14mm) has 2 dark thoracic stripes, reddish eyes and a cream abdomen. **BIOLOGY:** Adults feed on exudates, including from faeces, and transmit various diseases. Maggots feed on fresh manure and rotting vegetable matter. **HABITAT:** Ubiquitous around stables and dwellings.

### Tsetse flies

Family Glossinidae
**wingspan 20–25mm** Only 4 spp. in SA; large, superficially like house flies (above), but with wings folded neatly on top of one another, and a long proboscis that swells into a bulb where it joins the head. *Glossina* sp. (wingspan 25mm) shown is brown, fairly large, and rests in an alert posture. **BIOLOGY:** Tsetse flies feed on mammals' blood. Notorious for transmitting the organism causing sleeping sickness. **HABITAT:** Tropical grassland and deep forest, depending on species.

## Louse flies
Family Hippoboscidae

**wingspan 16–25mm** 37 spp. in SA; medium-sized, flattened, leathery. The Cattle louse fly *Hippobosca rufipes* (shown, wingspan 25mm) is dark red, patterned with triangular ivory patches. Wings fold like scissor blades over the back. **BIOLOGY:** Ectoparasitic, feeding on the blood of mammals and birds. Scuttle rapidly through fur or feathers. **HABITAT:** Ubiquitous; some live on pigeons in cities, others on sheep.

## Bat flies (bat louse flies)
Family Nycteribiidae

**length 3–6mm** 16 spp. in SA; bizarre, spider-like, wingless. Eyes reduced or absent. *Pencillidia fulvida* (shown, length 3mm) has very strong orange legs and a small head sunken into the flesh-coloured body. **BIOLOGY:** Specialized parasites of bats. Females give birth to mature larvae on cave walls, the larvae pupating immediately. **HABITAT:** Pupae live on the walls of bat roosts, adults found among bat fur.

## Bluebottles, greenbottles and blowflies
Family Calliphoridae

**wingspan 10–30mm** Significant family, with >150 spp. in SA. Stout, medium-sized to large, brightly coloured metallic flies (the family name translates as 'beautiful fly'). Under magnification the terminal bristle of the antenna appears feather-like. Females are attracted to decaying animal matter, on which the larvae feed.

### Copper-tailed blowfly
*Chrysomya chloropyga*

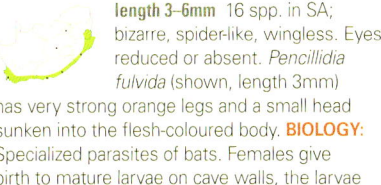

**wingspan 18mm** Medium-sized with metallic green, blue and copper bands. Thorax has a black marking resembling an inverted 'U'. **BIOLOGY:** Larvae develop in corpses, but can also attack damp, urine-stained tissue under the wool of sheep, causing large ulcers and death ('blowfly strike'). **HABITAT:** Ubiquitous, adults are quickly attracted to fresh corpses.

### Banded blowfly
*Lucilia sericata*

**wingspan 12mm** Familiar, metallic bronze-green household fly. **BIOLOGY:** Adults attracted by the odours of fish and meat, on which eggs are laid. Also cause blowfly strike on sheep, where they excrete ammonia that attracts even more flies. **HABITAT:** Very common in summer in and around households, the larvae developing in bin liners that contain scraps of meat and fish.

### Flesh flies

Family Sarcophagidae
**wingspan 15–28mm** >150 spp. in SA; large, robust; many have a grey-and-white striped thorax and a 'chequerboard' of light and dark abdominal patches. *Sarcophaga pachtyli* (shown, wingspan 28mm) has rows of 3 black dots on the abdomen. **BIOLOGY:** Larvae develop on rich organic matter, including faeces. *S. pachtyli* larvae are beneficial as they parasitize the egg cases of locusts and grasshoppers. **HABITAT:** Ubiquitous in urban areas; attracted to dog droppings.

### Tachinid flies

Family Tachinidae
**wingspan 10–25mm** Diverse family; ± 377 spp. in SA; medium-sized, stout, covered with very long, strong bristles. *Dejeania* sp. (wingspan 20mm) shown is yellow and orange, with dark wings and an inflated, bristly abdomen. **BIOLOGY:** All are beneficial for agriculture: they parasitize insect larvae – in the case of *Dejeania*, those of the Army bollworm *Helicoverpa armigera* (p.122). Flight loud, buzzing. **HABITAT:** Rest on understorey herbage in open woodland.

### Warble flies and botflies

Family Oestridae
**wingspan 15–20mm** 7 spp. in SA; large, unusual with big heads and mottled grey, bristle-free bodies. *Gedoelstia* sp. (wingspan 18mm) shown is pale, with a huge head and small, speckled abdomen. Barrel-shaped white larvae are covered with short spines. **BIOLOGY:** Adults short-lived and do not feed; larvae burrow into skin or the nasal passages of mammals, then emerge, or are sneezed out, and pupate in soil. **HABITAT:** Summer-rainfall region, where large mammal hosts occur.

J. Roff

### Horse botflies

Family Gasterophilidae
**wingspan 30mm** 12 spp. in SA; adults yellow, bee-like and lack mouthparts. Larvae (shown) stout and barrel-like, with rows of short black spines. **BIOLOGY:** Like Oestridae (above), adults are short-lived and rarely seen. Eggs are laid on a host's fur, and are then licked up during grooming and swallowed; larvae feed on the guts of the host, which can become packed with larvae. **HABITAT:** Widespread, especially in areas supporting herds of ungulates.

L.E.O Braack

# FLEAS

Order Siphonaptera

Very distinctive, small, strongly compressed (laterally flattened), completely wingless insects with keel-shaped heads for wriggling rapidly though the fur or feathers of their hosts. Body very hard and difficult to crush. Hindlegs larger than first 2 pairs of legs and able to generate spectacular leaps. Exclusively parasitic on birds or mammals. Females require a blood meal before laying eggs. Larvae are maggot-like and feed partially on the faeces of the adults. Pupae can remain dormant for months, hatching in response to vibrations produced by the presence of hosts. Fleas are of immense medical significance, notably as vectors for plague and typhus. They also act as intermediate hosts for tapeworms. Nearly 100 spp. in SA.

## Common fleas

Family Pucilidae

**length 1–3mm** Large and diverse family that includes 45 spp. in SA, among which are most of the significant pests of humans and their domestic animals.

### Cat flea

*Ctenocephalides felis*

**length 2–3mm** Abundant and widespread and the most common flea in human dwellings. **BIOLOGY:** Despite its name, infests dogs and humans, as well as cats. Adults are voracious blood feeders, injecting saliva with anticoagulant properties into wounds made with their piercing mouthparts, and causing irritation and swelling. Large white eggs fall to the ground and the larvae live in carpets and between floorboards, feeding on skin scales and flea faeces. Can transmit parasites and diseases, including tapeworms. **HABITAT:** Primarily in human dwellings.

## Jigger and sticktight fleas

Family Hectopsyllidae

**length 1–3mm** This small family of fleas includes only the Jigger and Sticktight fleas.

### Sticktight flea (Hen flea)

*Echidnophaga gallinacea*

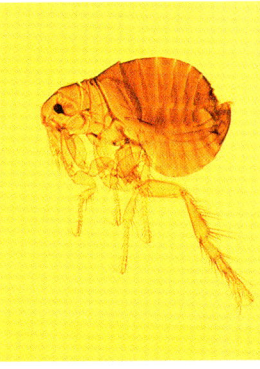

**length 2–3mm** Cosmopolitan flea found on a variety of birds and mammals and best recognized by its habits. **BIOLOGY:** Large numbers may accumulate around the eyes, wattles and combs of poultry, embedding deep into the skin, which becomes swollen and ulcerated. Eggs are laid in the ulcers and larvae drop to the ground, where they feed on organic debris. Infected birds exhibit reduced growth and egg production. A related species, *E. larina*, occurs on warthogs and bushpigs. **HABITAT:** The skin of host birds.

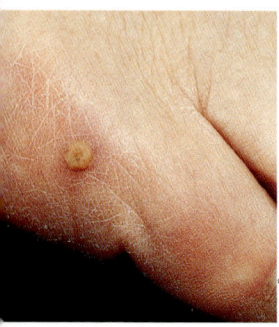

### Jigger (Chigoe flea) *Tunga penetrans*

**length 1–3mm** Native to Central and South America and introduced to the tropical areas of southern Africa. One of smallest fleas. **BIOLOGY:** Burrows into areas of soft skin, especially on the feet. As their eggs develop, females swell dramatically, sometimes causing intense irritation and creating a blister-like swelling with a central black dot – the exposed hind end of the flea itself. **HABITAT:** Females live in the skin of humans and other mammals; males leave the host after a blood meal and are free-living in sand.

## CADDISFLIES
**Order Trichoptera**

Adults resemble moths, but have hairs, not scales, on the wings and reduced chewing mouthparts, rather than a proboscis. The aquatic larvae are important components of freshwater food webs and have a range of feeding habits. Most construct silk retreats – portable or fixed – that may be ornamented with gravel or debris. Larvae have strong thoracic legs and a pair of hooks at the end of the abdomen; more commonly encountered than adults, and more readily identified to family level. Adults fly weakly and are attracted to lights. Eighteen families occur in SA.

### Web-spinning caddisflies
Family Hydropsychidae

**wingspan 44–56mm** Includes 23 spp. in SA; adults medium-sized with pale wings in shades of brown. Larvae often apple green, with tufted gills along the length of the body. *Chaematopsyche* larva shown (length 8mm). **BIOLOGY:** Larvae construct a retreat of small pebbles glued to rocks and then trap food particles with a net spun from silk. **HABITAT:** Common in fast-flowing streams and rivers.

### Long-horned caddisflies   Family Leptoceridae

**wingspan 20mm** >120 spp. in SA; adults slender, wings narrow, antennae very long, thin and held parallel in front of the body. *Athripsodes* larva shown (length 6mm). **BIOLOGY:** Larvae live and may swim in portable cases, often comprising strips of vegetation glued together with silk. Very sensitive to water pollution and hence good indicators of water quality. **HABITAT:** Found in fast-flowing streams, rivers, dams and vleis.

### Finger-net caddisflies   Family Philopotamidae

**wingspan 20mm** Includes 15 spp. in SA; adults (image left) have dark wings with a white spot on the leading edge, larvae (image right) often bright yellow. Adult and larval *Chimarra ambulans* shown (larval length 15mm). **BIOLOGY:** Adults scuttle over rocks in streams; larvae inhabit purse-like silk retreats. **HABITAT:** Fast-flowing mountain streams and rivers.

### Golden horn caddisflies
Family Hydrosalpingidae

**wingspan 20mm** A single sp. in SA; *Hydrosalpinx sericea* has larvae (shown) that construct tubes of golden-brown silk that are often found attached in clusters to rocks. **BIOLOGY:** Numbers appear to have dropped as a result of trout predation. **HABITAT:** Restricted to pristine streams in the mountains of the Western Cape.

## MOTHS AND BUTTERFLIES   Order Lepidoptera

Minute to very large, with large, membranous wings; body covered with flattened scales and hairs. Primarily plant-feeders; the mouthparts form a long, coiled proboscis. The larvae have additional pairs of prolegs along the abdomen, for firm attachment to vegetation. Over 660 butterfly and an estimated 11,000 moth species occur in SA.

**Moths (pp.107–122)** are usually nocturnal, with coupling hooks and bristles joining the fore- and hindwings. Moths have thread-like or branched antennae; wings generally fold in a roof-like position over the body. Small moths can be confused with caddisflies, but have scales, not hairs, on the wings and a proboscis, not chewing mouthparts. Moth pupae are generally protected in a silk cocoon.

**Butterflies (pp.123–129)** are diurnal, usually brightly coloured, and hold their wings upright at rest. Their antennae are always thin, usually ending in a club or curved hook. The pupae are naked.

### Swift moths (ghost moths)   Family Hepialidae

**wingspan 30–150mm** 80 spp. in SA; medium-sized to large; primitive, with short, thin antennae and large wings; fore- and hindwings coupled in flight by a forewing lobe. Silver-spotted ghost moth *Venus leto* (shown, wingspan 150mm) is large, iconic, pink-bodied, with silver-spotted maroon forewings. **BIOLOGY:** Its larvae take a few years to develop inside the trunk of a keurboom. **HABITAT:** *V. leto* found in indigenous forest.

### Longhorn moths
Family Adelidae

**wingspan 10–20mm** Includes at least 68 spp. in SA; small, drab moths with disproportionately long antennae. The small Dusted longhorn *Ceromitia turpisella* (shown, wingspan 15mm) is largely white, with 2 parallel black bands across the wings. **BIOLOGY:** Adults feed on nectar, larvae may 'mine' leaves, leaving meandering traceries across the leaf blade. A few species live in portable cases, like those of bagworms (p.109). **HABITAT:** Common across the region, attracted to lights.

### Goat moths (carpenter moths)
Family Cossidae

**wingspan 1–80mm** Includes ± 100 spp. in SA; medium-sized to large, heavily built moths with cryptically coloured wings. The Leopard goat *Azygophleps inclusa* (shown, wingspan 25–80mm) is variable in size, probably due to the fluctuating food quality available to the grub-like cream larvae. **BIOLOGY:** Larvae are destructive, boring into the heartwood of trees, where they take years to develop. **HABITAT:** Most common in open woodland and savanna; a few species are pests in urban areas, where their larvae feed on grass roots.

### Leaf rollers
Family Tortricidae

**wingspan 10–25mm** Includes 40 spp. in SA; small moths with rectangular, cryptically marked wings. The Coddling moth *Cydia pomonella* (shown, wingspan 16mm) is small, with a metallic copper ring at the tips of the grey wings. **BIOLOGY:** *C. pomonella* is a serious agricultural pest, as the grub-like pink larvae tunnel into apples and certain other fruit. **HABITAT:** Orchards in the Western Cape province.

## Flower moths
Family Scythrididae

**wingspan 10–14mm** Includes ± 6 spp. in SA; small, with narrow black wings marked with rows of yellow spots. *Eretmocera syleuta* (shown, wingspan 12mm) has red or yellow hindwings (hidden in this image) and antennae that are thick at the base, terminating in a thin, whip-like tip. **BIOLOGY:** Adults fly by day. Larval food plants are unknown, but possibly grasses. **HABITAT:** *E. syleuta* common in grassland and weedy areas in the summer-rainfall region.

## Bagworms
Family Psychidae

**wingspan 15–40mm** Includes ± 134 spp. in SA; the larvae and wingless adult females construct and live in bags of twigs and leaves. Adult males have stubby transparent wings, feathery antennae and lack mouthparts. The Wattle bagworm *Kotochalia bunodi* (larva shown, length 43 mm) is common in the eastern parts of the region. Adult male is black with clear wings lacking scales. **BIOLOGY:** Males locate wingless females in their cases, where they mate, leaving females to lay eggs in the case. **HABITAT:** Bagworms are common across the region, especially in open woodland and savanna.

## Clothes moths
Family Tineidae

**wingspan 10–25mm** Includes >100 spp. in SA; small moths with long grey or yellow wings fringed with long hairs. Proboscis is reduced or absent. The alien Case-bearing clothes moth *Tinea pellionella* (adult wingspan 10mm) is common indoors, where the larva (bottom image) lives in flattened portable cases and feeds destructively on wool and clothing. **BIOLOGY:** Family very diverse, most species feeding on enriched animal matter in birds' and mammals' nests, owl pellets, wool and the like. **HABITAT:** Native species are common in most habitats; all clothes moths occurs in buildings.

**MOTHS AND BUTTERFLIES**

### Clear-wing moths
Family Sesiidae

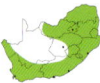

**wingspan 10–25mm** Includes 90 spp. in SA; small wasp mimics with clear wings and banded bodies. White-banded clear-wings of genus *Chamanthedon* (shown) are black with white bands on the abdomen, which terminates in a white brush. **BIOLOGY:** Very active by day, movements wasp-like. One species is a pest of rooibos plants. **HABITAT:** Widespread, but rarely encountered. Larvae bore into trees and shrubs.

### Ermine moths
Family Yponomeutidae

**wingspan 8–25mm** Includes 8 spp. in SA; medium-sized moths with pearl-grey or white wings evenly peppered with small black dots. The Speckled ermine *Yponomeuta fumigata* (shown, wingspan 20mm) has dark grey hindwings and gregarious, speckled larvae. **BIOLOGY:** Larvae feed in groups under extensive silk sheets on the trunks of their host trees, *Maytenus* and *Cassine* spp. **HABITAT:** A range of vegetation types from fynbos to subtropical forest.

### Grassland moths
Family Xyloryctidae

**wingspan 20–30mm** Includes a few regional species of cryptic moths with hindwings broader than the forewings, and with prominent palps projecting from the mouthparts. The Grassland moth *Eupetochira xystopala* (shown, wingspan 26mm) has silvery wings with a yellow stripe running down the centre. **BIOLOGY:** Larvae feed on leaves, lichens, nuts and fruit. Adult moths cryptic when resting on grass stems. **HABITAT:** Grassland.

### Concealer moths
Family Oecophoridae

**wingspan 20–30mm** A small family; drab, with rounded wing tips (or wingless) and a tuft of hairs at the base of each antenna. *Schiffermuelleria pedicata* (shown, wingspan 28mm) is small, with patterned orange wings and prominent palps extending from the mouthparts. **BIOLOGY:** Larvae often build cases of dry leaves bound with silk, but in some species larvae tunnel into wood or form galls. **HABITAT:** *S. pedicata* found in open woodland and urban areas.

**MOTHS AND BUTTERFLIES**

## Burnets and foresters
Family Zygaenidae

**wingspan 12–30mm** ± 100 spp. in SA; small, brightly coloured moths. Forewings metallic blue or green, with red bands or dots; antennae end in hooked clubs. Belted burnets of genus *Neurosymploca* (shown, wingspan 26mm) are grey with bright red dots on the wings. **BIOLOGY:** Larvae feed on a range of woody plants; the slow-flying, poisonous adults feed on flowers by day. **HABITAT:** Grassland and low open vegetation.

## Handmaidens, tiger moths and tussock moths
Family Erebidae

**wingspan 30–65mm** A recently constructed, very large family with few defining characteristics, but usually with broad forewings and patterned hindwings. Contains a large number of subfamilies, many of which were previously considered separate families.

### Tiger moths and footmen
Subfamily Arctiinae

**wingspan 20–60mm** Includes 300 spp. in SA; small to medium-sized moths. Body frequently has alternating yellow and black stripes, wings often brightly coloured. Larvae are the familiar 'woolly-bear caterpillars'. Tiger moths are more robust than the smaller, narrow-winged footmen. Most species are toxic.

### Tri-coloured tiger
*Rhodogastria amasis*

**wingspan 60mm** Medium-sized silver-white moth with bulky red-and-white abdomen; undersides of wings yellow, with small black crescents. Larvae large, covered with long black and ginger hairs. **BIOLOGY:** When touched, adults curl the abdomen upward, thus exposing their warning coloration. Larvae feed on a wide range of food plants. **HABITAT:** Various vegetation types, common in gardens.

### Crimson-speckled footman
*Utetheisa pulchella*

**wingspan 35mm** Medium-sized; forewings brightly speckled with red and black dots. Larvae yellow with black bands. **BIOLOGY:** Flies slowly by day. Larvae feed on grasses, plantain, Patterson's curse *Echium plantagineum*, and *Heliotropum* spp. **HABITAT:** Common across Africa in weedy areas and agricultural fields, wherever its food plants occur.

### Yellow-sleeved maiden  *Ceryx anthraciformes*

**wingspan 24mm** Small, with brown body; fore- and hindwings bluish-brown with orange patches. Larvae short, covered with long hairs. **BIOLOGY:** Sluggish and a poor flier. Larval food plant not known; larvae probably store plant toxins for self-defence. **HABITAT:** Bushveld in the summer-rainfall parts of the region.

### Heady maiden  *Amata cerbera*

**wingspan 30mm** Small, brightly coloured moth with bluish-green body and wings, the latter with clear panels. Abdomen banded with red or orange stripes. **BIOLOGY:** Sluggish and probably toxic. Larvae recorded feeding on a variety of trees and herbs, as well as on grass. **HABITAT:** Widespread; found from succulent karoo to the bushveld.

### Snouted tigers  Subfamily Aganainae

**wingspan 40–60mm** Similar to tiger moths, with 18 spp. in SA; antennae very thin; wings large and colourful. The Specious tiger moth *Asota speciosa* (shown, wingspan 60mm) has brown forewings marked with thin white lines and with orange patches at the wing bases; larva orange, with cream dorsal surface, which has black stripes and long, thin white hairs. **BIOLOGY:** Larval food plants comprise various figs and poison bushes, *Akocanthera* spp. **HABITAT:** Forest habitat and gardens with domestic fig trees.

### Tussock moths (gypsy moths)
Subfamily Lymantriinae

**wingspan 20–40mm** Over 300 spp. in SA; medium-sized moths with hairy body and wings, feathery antennae, reduced mouthparts and broad yellow-white wings. Powdered gypsy moth *Lacipa pulverea* shown (adult wingspan 11mm); its larva has 4 tufts of hair on the body. **BIOLOGY:** *L. pulverea* often attracted to lights. **HABITAT:** Various vegetation types.

**MOTHS AND BUTTERFLIES**

### African maiden moths  Family Thyretidae

**wingspan 25–50mm** Includes 33 spp. in SA; small, narrow-winged moths with reduced hindwings. Body is thin and hindwings may have clear windows. The Bar maiden *Thyretes caffra* (shown, wingspan 38mm) has grey wings with clear panels and a grey abdomen with a series of yellow dots. **BIOLOGY:** *T. caffra* larvae feed on the Sweet thorn *Acacia karoo*. **HABITAT:** *T. caffra* found in a variety of vegetation types from fynbos to forest.

### Slug moths  Family Limacodidae

**wingspan 20–30mm** Includes >120 spp. in SA. Squat, bristly larvae and easily recognized, plump, short-winged adults. Wings rounded, often emerald green but sometimes with brown or white markings. *Coenobasis* sp. (wingspan 26mm) shown has green wings and an orange abdomen. The green-and-yellow larvae are very short and broad, with small blue rings on the body, which sports branched stinging spines. Cocoon hard and oval, often glued to a wall. **BIOLOGY:** Larvae feed on wattle and other acacias and are capable of causing painful skin blisters. **HABITAT:** Most urban and native habitats.

### Diamond-backed moths  Family Plutellidae

**wingspan 10–15mm** Includes 10 spp. in SA; very small moths with narrow wings that have lighter inner margins, which, at rest, form a pale stripe running along the centre of the back. The Diamond-backed moth *Plutella xylostella* (shown, wingspan 12mm) has brown wings and a cream central stripe running along the body. Its larvae are green. **BIOLOGY:** *P. xylostella* is a cosmopolitan pest of cabbage, leaving transparent patches on damaged leaves. **HABITAT:** Agricultural land where cabbages are grown.

## Pyralid snout moths
Family Pyralidae

**wingspan 10–35mm** Includes 80 spp. in SA; small to large moths of variable appearance. Often lightly built, with very broad hindwings. Wings satiny and translucent. The larvae live in silken retreats and wriggle when disturbed. Many are pests of crops and stored products.

### Eldana borer (Sugar-cane borer)
*Eldana saccharina*

**wingspan 25mm** Adults smallish, wings brown and unmarked. Larvae brown and leathery. **BIOLOGY:** Adults are short-lived and lay eggs on sedges and sugar cane, into which the larvae bore. Causes severe crop losses of sugar cane, as the larvae are protected from insecticide applications. **HABITAT:** Found in wetlands and sugar cane in subtropical summer-rainfall areas.

### White pearl
*Palpita unionalis*

**wingspan 28mm** Smallish, with clear, opalescent white wings bordered on their leading edge by a thin gold stripe. Larvae pale green with fine white lateral hairs. **BIOLOGY:** Larvae feed on jasmine and olive species. Often attracted to lights. **HABITAT:** A widespread and common moth in gardens and natural vegetation.

### Dried fruit moths
*Ephestia* spp.

**wingspan 14mm** Small, drab grey moths with faint dark bands along the forewings. Larvae are small cream maggots. **BIOLOGY:** Pests of food products like biscuits, nuts, chocolate and dried fruit and often detected by larval webbing on stored foodstuffs. **HABITAT:** Ubiquitous in households – any small, slow-flying, grey moths in houses probably belong to this genus.

## Plume moths
Family Pterophoridae

**wingspan 10–20mm** Includes 70 spp. in SA; small, delicate moths with long legs and thin wings that are held outstretched. Wings have deep incisions, forming separate 'plumes'. Some roll their wings at rest and hold them forward, giving the body a T- or Y-shaped outline. The Orange plume moth *Crombrugghia wahlbergi* (shown, wingspan 14mm) has an orange body and wings. **BIOLOGY:** Pterophorid larvae often feed on daisy flowers. Adults fly slowly when disturbed. **HABITAT:** Weedy fields and rank grasses under trees.

## Many-plume moths
Family Alucitidae

**wingspan 10–15mm** Small family with wings split into approximately 12 feathery rods and held open like a fan. Adult Many-plume moth *Alucita spicifera* (shown, wingspan 12mm) has brown-and-white banded wings; the larvae are covered with long hairs. **BIOLOGY:** Alucitid adults feed on the nectar of weedy annual plants. **HABITAT:** Weedy fields and grass under trees in open woodland.

## Geometrid moths
Family Geometridae

**wingspan 20–55mm** Very large family (1,000 spp. in SA) of moths with small bodies and very large, cryptically coloured wings held outstretched and flat against the substrate at rest. The elongate larvae (known as 'loopers', 'inchworms' or 'measuring worms') have few prolegs (additional legs) on the body and move by pulling the last part of the body forward to touch the thoracic legs, forming a 'loop' and then extending again.

### Oblique peacock
*Chiasmia simplicilinea*

**wingspan 32mm** Medium-sized moth with a single, continuous dark brown horizontal stripe across the pale brown wings, which are held outstretched at rest. Hindwings triangular. Larvae are pale green loopers with fine white markings. **BIOLOGY:** Larvae feed on wattle trees; adults are known to suck lachrymal fluid from the eyes of livestock. **HABITAT:** Agricultural land and a range of natural habitats.

### Dusters
*Pingasa* spp.

**wingspan 40mm** Heavily built moths with grey-and-green speckling over the white wings and body; larvae are thick green loopers with a pale yellow stripe running along sides of the body. **BIOLOGY:** Larval food plants are cabbage trees *Cussonia*, Natal plums *Carissa* and alien pepper trees *Schinus* spp. **HABITAT:** Open woodland and forest; commonly seen at rest on tree trunks and under large leaves.

### Cycad looper
*Zerenopsis lepida*

**wingspan 40mm** Medium-sized moth with bright orange wings covered with large black dots. Larvae (bottom image) are orange, heavily marked with thin, black transverse lines. **BIOLOGY:** One of the few moth species to feed on cycads, often causing extensive defoliation. Larvae also feed on wild plums *Carissa* and wild pears *Apodytes* spp. **HABITAT:** Found largely in forest, but also in gardens.

### Red-lined emerald
*Heterorachis devocata*

**wingspan 22mm** Small, fragile moth with pale green wings with dull red marginal stripes. Abdomen is red dorsally. **BIOLOGY:** Larval food plants are wild alders *Vangueria* spp. and wild medlars *Canthium* spp. **HABITAT:** A common moth in a variety of habitats, especially woodland and forest.

**MOTHS AND BUTTERFLIES**

# Emperor moths
Family Saturniidae

**wingspan 50–160mm** 74 spp. in SA; spectacular, large moths with equally impressive, bulky larvae, which change colour with every moult. Most have eyespots or clear, crescent-shaped panels on the wings. Antennae of males are comb-like. Forewings often end in curved tips. Adults do not feed, living only a few days. In some species, the larvae construct cocoons in which to pupate, in others the pupa is bare and develops in soil.

## Gold-marbled emperor *Tagoropsis flavinata*

**wingspan 93mm** Large bright yellow moth with a thin brown line and wavy patches on the wings. Forewings with single, small eyespot. Larvae black, with many thin white longitudinal stripes and orange spiny protuberances projecting from the body. **BIOLOGY:** Larvae feed on the African false currant *Allophylus africanus*. **HABITAT:** Open subtropical woodland and forest.

## Zigzag emperor (Willow emperor)
*Imbrasia tyrrhea*

**wingspan 120mm** Large; wings fawn with pale pink eyespots and black zigzagging lines bordered in white. Larvae black, but heavily speckled with patches of white and red scales. **BIOLOGY:** As with other emperor moths, most commonly seen at lights. Larvae feed on various species of acacia and on willow and apple trees. **HABITAT:** A variety of vegetation types.

## Luna moth (Moon moth) *Argema mimosae*

**wingspan 120mm** Large and unmistakable with its yellow-green wings and long streamers on the hindwings. All wings have yellow-ringed brown eyespots. Larvae pale green, with vertical yellow bands and blue markings on each segment. Pupate in silvery cocoons. **BIOLOGY:** Cocoon pitted with small holes, presumably to deter wasps by mimicking a cocoon already parasitized. **HABITAT:** Found in subtropical bushveld.

## Mopane moth
*Imbrasia belina*

**wingspan 120mm** Large and familiar fawn-coloured moth with orange eyespots on the hindwings and brown and white bands across both wings. Larvae black, but heavily speckled with patches of alternating bluish-white, red and yellow scales. **BIOLOGY:** Larvae feed on a wide range of trees and shrubs and are a major food source for humans in certain areas. **HABITAT:** In nearly every vegetation type across the region. Most abundant in the arid summer-rainfall region.

## Monkey moths (giant lappet moths)
Family Eupterotidae

**wingspan 30–100mm** ± 75 spp. in SA. Large moths with big, rounded wings fringed with hairs. Wings are subdued shades of brown, but have a silky sheen. *Jana tantalus* (shown, wingspan 100mm) has grey forewings and pale brown bars on the hindwings. Body bulky and covered with long hairs. **BIOLOGY:** *J. tantalus* larvae feed on the Septee saucer berry *Cordia caffra* and wild jasmines *Jasminium* spp. **HABITAT:** Open woodland and forest.

## Eggar moths (lappet moths)
Family Lasiocampidae

**wingspan 25–100mm** >150 spp. in SA; fairly large, heavily built, hairy moths lacking a proboscis. Forewings long and narrow, hindwings reduced and rounded. The Cape lappet *Eutricha capensis* (shown, wingspan 70mm) has reddish-brown forewings dusted with white scales and bearing wavy white bands. Larvae have a black stripe running along the body, bordered with bright orange bristles. **BIOLOGY:** Larvae are seen in groups on the trunks of their food plants (acacias, White stinkwood *Celtis africana* and a range of alien trees). **HABITAT:** Various vegetation types, also common in gardens.

# Hawk moths (sphinx moths)　　　　　　　　　Family Sphingidae

**wingspan 25–140mm** >100 spp. in SA; large, streamlined moths with a heavily built abdomen and short, narrow, pointed wings. Eyes large and proboscis very long. Powerful fliers that hover while feeding from tubular flowers. Larvae smooth, with a thin horn at the end of the body.

## Death's-head hawk moth　　*Acherontia atropos*

**wingspan 110mm** Body large and bulky with skull-like markings on the thorax. Forewings mottled grey and brown, hindwings with yellow base. Larval coloration varied, usually yellow-green with grey or purple chevrons on each segment. **BIOLOGY:** Adults raid beehives for honey, producing a squeaking noise via their breathing tubes ('trachea') to mimic sounds made by the queen bee. Larvae feed on various plants, including grapevines and potatoes. **HABITAT:** Common in urban areas and in most vegetation types.

## Silver-striped hawk moth　　*Hippotion celerio*

**wingspan 75mm** Body large, buff-coloured, with thin white lines running along the length of the forewings. Hindwings with pink bases. Larvae green or brown, with a prominent pair of eyespots on the thorax. **BIOLOGY:** Adults capable of long migrations. Larvae feed on various plants, including grapevines, arum lilies, impatiens, carrots and herbs. **HABITAT:** Very common in gardens and in most vegetation types.

## African hummingbird hawk moth
*Macroglossum trochilus*

**wingspan 40mm** Small, light brown moths with prominent patches of black scales sticking out of the sides of the abdomen and forming a fan; hindwings orange with yellow bases. **BIOLOGY:** Adults very rapid fliers, often seen hovering accurately in front of tubular nectar flowers. **HABITAT:** Common in gardens where larval food plants (the alien mirror bush, *Coprosma repens*) and adult nectar bushes (lavender, basil, salvias) occur.

**MOTHS AND BUTTERFLIES**

### Oriental bee hawk *Cephonodes hylas*

**wingspan 70mm** Medium-sized, wings clear with black veins, body mustard-yellow, abdomen has brown band halfway along its length and ends in a retractable tuft of hairs. Larvae thin, body yellow or green, with a black line running along the sides and with short, vertical black-and-white bars. **BIOLOGY:** Larval food plants are the Wild pomegranate *Burchellia bubalina*, coffee and other shrubs. Adults spread the abdominal fan while feeding. **HABITAT:** Widepread across many vegetation types, but never common.

### Prominents (puss moths) Family Notodontidae

**wingspan 40–60mm** >200 spp. in SA; medium-sized moths with a ridge running along the centre of the body, best seen in side view. Larvae very diverse in appearance, sometimes with inflated, gecko-like heads. As with all adult prominent moths, the Imitating bufftip *Phalera imitata* (shown, wingspan 56mm) is superbly camouflaged, with buff-tipped grey wings. **BIOLOGY:** Notodontid adults often mimic the stump of a broken twig. **HABITAT:** *P. imitata* occurs in open woodland and subtropical forest.

### Processionary moths Family Thaumetopoeidae

**wingspan 40–50mm** 6 spp. in SA; medium-sized moths with comb-like antennae and a tuft of hair at the end of the abdomen. Reticulate bagnet *Anaphe reticulata* (shown, wingspan 42mm) has silvery wings patterned with bold, geometric brown lines. **BIOLOGY:** Its gregarious larvae attract attention as they migrate to new food plants (the Wild pear *Dombeya rotundifilia*) in processions, with contact maintained between the individuals. They pupate together in one large purse-like 'bagnet'. **HABITAT:** Bushveld and subtropical forest.

**MOTHS AND BUTTERFLIES**

## Forester moths
Family Agaristidae

**wingspan 50–60mm** 50 spp. in SA; medium-sized, brightly coloured moths with thin antennae; capable of sound production. Larvae brightly coloured, with a hump at the end of the body. Trimen's false tiger *Agoma trimenii* (shown, wingspan 54mm) has cream-and-brown forewings and orange hindwings. **BIOLOGY:** Its slow-flying adults sport warning coloration and are probably toxic. Larval food plants are wild grapes, *Rhoicissus* and *Cissus* spp. **HABITAT:** Subtropical forest.

## Owlet moths
Family Noctuidae

**wingspan 15–100mm** The largest moth family, includes 1,700 spp. in SA. Forewings usually triangular and cryptically coloured, hindwings plainer, antennae thin. Their larvae include the well-known cutworms, army worms and bollworms. Pupation occurs in the soil, with or without a flimsy silken cocoon.

### Golden plusia

*Trichoplusia orichalcea*

**wingspan 40mm** Medium-sized with a bright metallic gold triangle on the forewings. Larvae green or blue-green semiloopers (they arch the body when moving) covered with fine white lines. **BIOLOGY:** Larvae feed destructively on a range of vegetables. **HABITAT:** Most common in agricultural and garden settings.

### Tomato moth (Cotton leafworm)
*Spodoptera littoralis*

**wingspan 37mm** Medium-sized moth, forewings brown, covered with fine geometric markings, wing tips with grey patch. Larvae greyish-brown cutworms, with pale yellow line running along the top of the body. **BIOLOGY:** A major pest on a variety of vegetable crops, but also feeds on hibiscus, lantana and eucalyptus. **HABITAT:** Ubiquitous across most habitats, including gardens and cropland.

### Army bollworm
*Helicoverpa armigera*

**wingspan 36mm** Medium-sized with fawn-coloured wings and body, hindwings cream with black border. Larvae grey-green, with black stripe running along the back and cream stripes running along the sides. **BIOLOGY:** Feeds on a range of crop plants, especially tomatoes. **HABITAT:** A ubiquitous, cosmopolitan pest.

### Sundowner moth
*Sphingomorpha chlorea*

**wingspan 60mm** Large, heavily built moth with intricately marked brown forewings and a cream stripe through the thorax. The well-camouflaged larvae have black-ringed yellow and red spots near the head and arch the body at rest. **BIOLOGY:** Larvae gregarious, feeding on acacias and other woodland trees, adults attracted to fermenting fruit, tree gum and alcoholic drinks. **HABITAT:** Common in bushveld and forest.

### Peach moth
*Egybolis vaillantina*

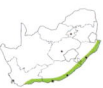

**wingspan 50mm** Medium-sized moth, wings metallic green-blue with striking orange markings. Larva grey-black with yellow and black rings along the body. **BIOLOGY:** Larval food plants include peach, soapberry *Sapindus* spp. and cotton. Adults fly slowly in the tree canopy by day. **HABITAT:** Subtropical bush and forest, extending up to Central Africa.

G. Branch

### Cream-striped owl
*Cyligramma latona*

**wingspan 75mm** Large brown moth with large eyespot on leading edge of forewing and cream stripe running diagonally across each wing. **BIOLOGY:** Wings held outstretched when at rest. Adults often attracted to lights or overripe fruit; green larvae feed on acacia *Senegalia* spp. **HABITAT:** Commonly seen in open bushveld, forest and grassland.

# Skippers
*Family Hesperiidae*

**wingspan 20–60mm** ± 130 spp. in SA. Small to medium-sized primitive butterflies, usually drab in colour, and active by day and at dusk. Wings often held half-open at rest. Common name of family refers to their characteristic quick, darting flight. Many species feed on grasses, palms and bananas, with larvae inhabiting leaves that are folded into tubes using silken threads.

## Sandmen
*Spialia* spp.

**wingspan 25mm** Genus with 14 very similar spp. in SA, all with dark wings bearing an array of white spots. Larvae black, with 2 interrupted yellow stripes running along sides of the body. **BIOLOGY:** Adults are fast fliers, often settling on open ground. Larvae feed on hibiscus and doll's roses *Hermmania* spp. **HABITAT:** Common, especially in areas of bare ground.

## Two-pip policeman
*Coeliades pisistratus*

**wingspan 50mm** Medium-sized and heavily built, wings greyish brown dorsally, brown with a white patch and 3 black spots ventrally, hindwings with orange tips. Larva banded in white and black, with large, black-spotted, yellow head capsule. **BIOLOGY:** Adults fly strongly at dawn and dusk. Larvae feed on a variety of plants, including bush willows *Combretum* spp. and the alien Bug tree *Solanum mauritianum*. **HABITAT:** The edges of subtropical forest and open woodland.

## Brush-footed butterflies
*Family Nymphalidae*

Very large family, with ± 180 spp. in SA. Forelegs reduced. Subfamilies include the monarchs, acraeas, browns, brush-foots and charaxes.

## Monarchs (milkweed butterflies)
*Subfamily Danainae*

**wingspan 50–90mm** Large, toxic butterflies with warning coloration. Larvae also brightly coloured, bearing 2–3 pairs of whip-like extensions along the body; they usually feed on milkweeds in the Asclepiadaceae family.

## Friar
*Amauris niavius*

**wingspan 80mm** Large butterfly, wings white with black veins and margins. Larva black with white bands along first and last part of the body, middle section banded in yellow, 3 pairs of whip-like projections on top of the body. **BIOLOGY:** Larval food plant is the Cowplant *Gymnema sylvestre*. Adults are slow fliers. **HABITAT:** Coastal and montane forest.

### African monarch
*Danaus chrysippus*

**wingspan 60mm** Familiar butterfly with orange-brown wings, bordered with black-and-white markings. Larvae strikingly banded in black, yellow and white, with 3 pairs of whip-like projections on top of the body. **BIOLOGY:** Adults toxic; slow-flying. Larval food plants comprise various milkweeds, especially *Asclepias* spp. **HABITAT:** Ubiquitous in most natural and disturbed habitats.

### Acraeas
Subfamily Acraeinae

**wingspan 30–60mm** Medium-sized butterflies, wings long, usually orange-red with black dots. Larvae dark-bodied, covered with branched spines. Pupae bright yellow and black, suspended head-down by a silken pad.

### Dusky acraea
*Hyalites esebria*

**wingspan 55mm** Medium-sized, wings dark brown with variable yellow or orange patches. **BIOLOGY:** Adults slow-flying, settling often. Larval food plants are stinging nettles *Urtica* spp. and a range of other herbaceous plants. **HABITAT:** Common in clearings and paths in montane and coastal forest.

### Garden acraea
*Acraea horta*

**wingspan 50mm** The commonest garden butterfly, with wings red (in male, shown) or orange (in female), dotted with black spots and with clear tips. Larvae (bottom image) almost metallic black, covered with branched spines. **BIOLOGY:** Slow-flying, often seen basking on leaves. Stops moving when caught. Larval food plants include the wild peaches *Kiggelaria* spp. and, occasionally, granadillas. **HABITAT:** Very common in forests and gardens.

## Browns
Subfamily Satyrinae

**wingspan 35–80mm** Small to medium-sized, dull brown butterflies, undersides of wings often with eyespots along their margins. Wing veins swollen at the base of the wings. Larvae green, grey or yellow, with a forked appendage at the end of the body; feed mainly on grasses and sedges.

### Table Mountain beauty *Aeropetes tulbaghia*

**wingspan 75mm** Large butterfly, upper sides of wings attractively patterned in brown and bright yellow, with a row of blue dots on hindwing margin. Larvae tan, with a row of small dots along sides of the body. **BIOLOGY:** Pollinate red flowers, including the Red disa *Disa uniflora*, red-hot pokers and watsonias. Larvae feed on various grasses. **HABITAT:** Mountains, occasionally straying into gardens and the city of Cape Town.

### Rainforest brown *Cassionympha cassius*

**wingspan 65mm** Medium-sized, with orange blotches and yellow-ringed eyespot on upper wing. Larvae are green, becoming maroon when older. **BIOLOGY:** Flight skipping; frequents forest paths and clearings. Larval food plants include grasses and the sedge *Pentaschistis capensis*. **HABITAT:** Coastal bush and montane forest.

### Twilight brown (Evening brown)
*Melanitis leda*

**wingspan 65mm** Large, upper side of wings brown with orange tip, underside camouflaged in greys and browns. Larva green, with a pair of maroon horns on the head and a forked structure at the rear. **BIOLOGY:** Adults rest on the ground in the open, becoming more active at dusk. Larval food plants comprise various grasses, including the Broad-leaved forest grass *Setaria megaphylla*. **HABITAT:** Coastal and montane forest, bush and woodland.

**MOTHS AND BUTTERFLIES**

## Swallowtails
Family Papilionidae

**wingspan 60–85mm** Very large, brightly marked butterflies, often with 'tails' on the hindwings. When alarmed, larvae can extrude a special forked scent gland (the 'osmetrium') from the head, releasing a foul odour.

### Citrus swallowtail
*Papilio demodocus*

**wingspan 85mm** Large butterfly, wings dark with bright yellow patches, hindwings lack tails; young larva resembles a shiny bird dropping, but becomes green and brown when older. **BIOLOGY:** In gardens, larvae feed on citrus, but in their natural habitat on citrus relatives in the Rutaceae family. **HABITAT:** Very common in gardens, also found in most moderately moist vegetation types.

### Mocker swallowtail
*Papilio dardanus*

**wingspan 85mm** Male yellow with black edges to the forewings and long tails on the hindwings. Female variable, lacking tails on hindwings and mimicking the toxic African monarch (p.124) or Friar (p.123) butterflies. **BIOLOGY:** Fly slowly along forest edges. A single female can produce offspring of both mimetic forms. **HABITAT:** Montane and coastal forest.

## Whites, sulphurs and orange tips
Family Pieridae

**wingspan 30–60mm** ± 46 spp. in SA; medium-sized, mainly white, yellow or orange, often with contrasting red or purple wing tips. Larvae smooth, with fine longitudinal stripes, generally feeding on Brassicaceae (cabbages, etc.) and Capparidaceae (caper plants).

### Scarlet tip
*Colotis danae*

**wingspan 44mm** Medium-sized; colour varies between sexes and with season. In dry season the male's wings are white, with black-edged red tips and black posterior spots. In wet season, the black areas enlarge. Wings of females have more black markings and, sometimes, yellow tips. Larvae covered with fine fuzzy hair; olive-green with a cream line running along the top of the body. **BIOLOGY:** Adults settle frequently on the ground; larvae feed on the Broad bean *Maurea angolensis* and the Natal worm-bush *Cadaba natalensis*. **HABITAT:** Savanna and thornveld vegetation.

### Meadow white
*Pontia helice*

**wingspan 38mm** Medium-sized butterfly, upper wing surfaces white with black markings at the apexes and margins (more pronounced in females). Underside heavily marked in yellow, grey and black. **BIOLOGY:** Flight rapid, settles often on nectar plants. Larval food plants are flaxes *Heliophila* spp. and other herbs. **HABITAT:** Widespread in fallow fields and grassland.

### Brown-veined white
*Belenois aurota*

**wingspan 45mm** Medium-sized, upper surface of wings white with black lines at apexes, especially in females; underside of wings white with brown-black lines along the wing veins. Larvae green, with 2 brown stripes running along sides of the body. **BIOLOGY:** Larval food plant is the Shepherds' tree *Boscia albitrunca*. **HABITAT:** Widespread, especially in more arid parts.

### Brush-foots
Subfamily Nymphalinae

**wingspan 40–75mm** Small to large, often brightly coloured butterflies. Forelegs reduced and non-functional. Larvae also diverse, often armed with branched spines.

### Diadem
*Hypolimnas misippus*

**wingspan 70mm** Large butterfly; upper wing surface brown in female and black with violet-edged white spots in male. Female mimics the African monarch (p.124). **BIOLOGY:** Larval food plants are the Wild foxglove *Asystasia gagentia* and succulent wild portulacas, *Talinum* spp. **HABITAT:** Open woodland and fallow fields.

### Garden inspector
*Junonia archesia*

**wingspan 50mm** Medium-sized butterfly, upper wings brown. Dry season form has broad reddish band along wing margins, and suffused purple wingtip; wet season form has dull yellow band running along wing margins. **BIOLOGY:** Larvae feed on the herbs *Coleus* and on spur plants, *Plectranthus* spp. **HABITAT:** Open rocky grassland, forest and gardens.

### Painted lady
*Cythia cardui*

**wingspan 45mm** Medium-sized butterfly, upper wing surface marbled with orange-pink and black spots, with a concentration of black and white spots on the wing tips. Larvae black, covered with fine spines. **BIOLOGY:** Cosmopolitan, with powerful flight. Larvae feed on a variety of plants. **HABITAT:** Ubiquitous in most habitats including gardens.

### Charaxes
Subfamily Charaxinae

**wingspan 40–80mm** Medium-sized to large, robust butterflies, with stout thorax and hard, strong wings, often covered with intricate designs. In Foxy charaxes *Charaxes jasius* (shown, wingspan 75mm) upper wing surface is orange, marked with black; underside has hieroglyphic-like markings. Larva smooth, with small fork-like projections at the rear and larger horns on the head. **BIOLOGY:** Fast and powerful fliers. *C. jasius* is attracted to sap oozing from wounds in tree trunks. **HABITAT:** It frequents open woodland and bushveld.

### Blues and coppers
Family Lycaenidae

**wingspan 11–50mm** ± 323 spp. in SA; a very diverse group of small butterflies with metallic blue, orange or brown upper wing surfaces. Larvae stubby; those of many species engage in a complex mutualistic relationship with ants: the ants feed on honeydew secreted by the larvae, which are then allowed access to the ants' nests, where they feed on ant larvae.

### Common opal
*Chrysoritis thysbe*

**wingspan 30mm** Small butterfly, upper wing surface bright orange with pale blue wing base. Larvae olive-green, stubby and covered with fine white hairs. **BIOLOGY:** Flies close to the ground, settling on rocks and bare ground. Initially, larvae are fed on various shrubs, including tick berries *Chrysanthemoides* spp.; thereafter they spend their time in the nests of cocktail ants (p.139). **HABITAT:** Typically coastal dunes, sometimes mountain tops.

### Common hairtail *Anthene definata*

**wingspan 27mm** Small butterfly, upper surface of wings purple-blue in male and paler blue in female, underside of wings grey, paler in female, with intricate wavy markings. Have 2 small orange and black dots at rear margin of the hindwings, plus short, thread-like tails. **BIOLOGY:** Larvae feed on acacias, *Vachellia* spp., and are often attended by ants seeking honeydew. **HABITAT:** Varied vegetation types, from coastal fynbos to hill slopes in bushveld.

## SAWFLIES, WASPS, BEES AND ANTS  Order Hymenoptera

An extremely diverse, abundant and ecologically important group, second only in species number to the beetles (p.66). Range in size from tiny to very large; have 2 pairs of membranous wings coupled in flight by a row of tiny hooks along the front edge of the hindwings. Almost all have a pronounced waist between thorax and abdomen. Most have biting mouthparts, frequently modified for sucking liquids. The egg-laying tube ('ovipositor') is often modified for boring, piercing or stinging. Many species form complex social groups. Ants are hugely important nutrient recyclers; bees and wasps play vital economic roles as pollinators, while parasitic wasps control many other insect populations.

### Sawflies  Family Tenthredinidae

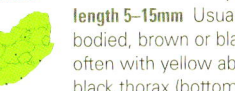

**length 5–15mm** Usually stout-bodied, brown or black insects, often with yellow abdomen and black thorax (bottom image); legs yellow and wings smoky. Lack the 'wasp waist' typical of most other hymenopterans. **BIOLOGY:** Adults sluggish. Females use the saw-like ovipositor to cut slits into leaves or stems, into which single eggs are laid. Larvae caterpillar- or slug-like and feed on vegetation. Some are significant pests, including the Pear-slug *Caliroa cerasi* (length 10mm, top image), a pest of plum and pear trees. **HABITAT:** A range of vegetation types; also in gardens.

## Woodwasps (horntails)
Family Siricidae

**length 20–30mm** Small family; 3 introduced spp. in SA. Mainly black-and-yellow or red wasps with the abdomen extended into a strong projecting spike (hence the name 'horntails'). **BIOLOGY:** Females drill into trees using the long ovipositor. Larvae long-lived and bore into wood. The Sirex woodwasp *Sirex noctilio* (shown, length 25mm) is a striking bluish-black with orange legs. A significant pest of pine plantations, it causes losses of over R300 million annually. **HABITAT:** Siricidae frequent pine forests in the southwestern Cape.

## Ichneumon wasps
Family Ichneumonidae

**length 12–25mm** Extremely diverse family with >500 spp. in SA; mostly medium-sized, slender-bodied parasitic wasps with long antennae and a long, curved abdomen. Females often have very long ovipositors. *Enicospilus* sp. (length 18mm) shown. **BIOLOGY:** Eggs usually laid directly into the bodies of hosts, which include the larvae of butterflies and moths, beetles, flies and other wasps. Some drill into wood to inject eggs directly into the bodies of wood-boring larvae. **HABITAT:** Diverse, but always associated with host insects.

## Braconid wasps
Family Braconidae

**length 3–38mm** Extremely diverse family of parasitic wasps, including several hundred described and many more undescribed species in SA. Generally smaller and stouter than ichneumonids (above), black, orange or red in colour, females often with extremely long ovipositors. **BIOLOGY:** Parasitize the larvae and pupae of butterflies and wasps, beetles, flies and bugs, especially aphids. Larvae emerging from an infected caterpillar spin silken cocoons on its body. *Charops* sp. (length 12mm) shown parasitizes mature caterpillars. **HABITAT:** Braconid wasps are ubiquitous across the region, including in urban settings.

**SAWFLIES, WASPS, BEES AND ANTS**

### Ensign wasps
Family Evanidae

**length 5–14mm** Distinctive wasps with disproportionately small, triangular or semicircular abdomen, compressed sideways and held upright via a narrow waist. The abdomen is constantly jerked up and down. Legs long, especially the last pair, usually black. *Evania* sp. (length 10mm) shown. **BIOLOGY:** Adults feed on nectar. Larvae develop inside oothecae of cockroaches. As cockroaches are most abundant around human habitation, often seen in and around houses, looking for victims to parasitize. **HABITAT:** *Evania* sp. in wooded areas and gardens.

### Carrot wasps
Family Gasteruptiidae

**length 8–25mm** ± 40 spp. in SA; relatively small, slender, usually reddish-brown wasps with a distinct 'neck' and very large eyes. Abdomen arises from high up on the thorax and expands gradually towards its tip. Tibiae of hindlegs are narrow at the base and swollen at the end. Female has extremely long ovipositor, often with a white tip. *Gasteruption* sp. (length 15mm) shown. **BIOLOGY:** Parasitize the nests of solitary wasps and bees, especially those of wood-boring species, such as carpenter bees. **HABITAT:** Rarely seen, but occur in most vegetation types.

### Fig wasps
Family Agaonidae

**length 1–4mm** Tiny wasps, best known for their close association with figs. Females dark, with strong chewing mandibles, strong hindlegs and wings with very few veins. Males pale, lacking wings and with the abdomen curved under the thorax. **BIOLOGY:** Males are flightless and never leave fig fruit. Females (shown) fly to new figs, carrying pollen with them and laying their eggs in the developing ovaries of female flowers. Each fig species hosts different wasps. **HABITAT:** Wherever wild figs occur, but most common in summer-rainfall areas.

**SAWFLIES, WASPS, BEES AND ANTS**

## Chalcidid wasps
Family Chalcidiidae

**length 3–7mm** Tiny, robust parasitic wasps, most easily recognized by the swollen femora on the hindlegs, which often bear a row of teeth along the lower margin. Body generally black with red or yellow markings, wings usually clear, with reduced venation. **BIOLOGY:** They parasitize the larvae and pupae of butterflies, moths and flies. *Brachymeria kassalensis* (shown, length 6mm) is typical and parasitizes the pupating larvae of *Acraea* butterflies. **HABITAT:** Forest, bush and gardens.

## Pteromalid wasps
Family Pteromalidae

**length 3–5mm** Diverse family of small, generally dumpy, brown to black parasitic wasps with a thick abdomen. Most parasitize other insects, but some form plant galls. The Acacia gall wasp *Trichilogaster acaciaelongifoliae* (shown, length 3mm) was deliberately introduced from Australia to control seed production in long-leaved wattle trees. **BIOLOGY:** Larval feeding causes flower buds to form round, green to orange galls, rather than flowers, within which the wasps develop. **HABITAT:** Frequent the Wattle tree *Acacia longifolia*.

## Cuckoo wasps
Family Chrysididae

**length 4–20mm** Diverse family of often spectacularly coloured metallic green, blue or red wasps with extremely hard, strongly sculptured bodies. *Chrysis concinna* (length 12mm) shown. **BIOLOGY:** Often curl into a ball when attacked. Typically associated with solitary bees and wasps, which they parasitize. Adult wasps lay eggs in the nest of a host species; their developing young consume the eggs and larvae of the host, as well as food provided by the host for its own larvae. **HABITAT:** Widespread and most often seen on the mud walls of deserted farmhouses, where they seek out wasps' nests constructed in crevices in the walls.

SAWFLIES, WASPS, BEES AND ANTS

## Mammoth wasps
Family Scoliidae

**length 10–50mm** Medium-sized to large, solitary wasps, usually black with yellow or orange hairs or markings. Wings often smoky, with fine longitudinal corrugations, especially toward the tips. Space between first and second abdominal segments is constricted. *Scolia wahlbergi* (length 30mm) shown. **BIOLOGY:** Parasitize scarab beetle larvae. Females burrow into soil to find beetle larvae, which they paralyse, before depositing a single egg on its body. Developing larva feeds externally, before pupating in soil. **HABITAT:** Low-growing vegetation and compost heaps.

## Tiphiid wasps
Family Tiphiidae

**length 4–30mm** Small to medium-sized, solitary wasps; males and females differ. Males elongate and slender with very long antennae, frequently attractively banded in black and white or black and yellow, often with an upturned hook at tip of the abdomen. Females heavier, and sometimes wingless. *Mesa* sp. (length 15mm) shown is common on flowering trees. **BIOLOGY:** Adult tiphiids feed on nectar. Females hunt on the ground for beetle larvae, which they paralyse before laying an egg on the victim. **HABITAT:** Occur in grassland and urban settings, where host beetles are abundant.

## Velvet ants
Family Mutillidae

**length 3–18mm** Large family, with hundreds of species in SA; wingless females resemble ants, males winged and often differently coloured from more frequently encountered females, which have extremely hard, coarsely punctured bodies, usually covered with soft, velvety hairs. Colour generally black, with various white, red or yellow bands and spots. *Mutilla astarte* female (length 12mm) shown. **BIOLOGY:** Velvet ants parasitize the larvae of bees, wasps and sometimes flies. Females inflict very painful stings. Adults feed on nectar. **HABITAT:** Common across the region, usually running on the ground in the heat of the day.

**SAWFLIES, WASPS, BEES AND ANTS**

### Spider wasps
Family Pompilidae

**length 7–50mm** Diverse family of active, long-legged, medium-sized to large, solitary wasps, usually with curled antennae. Most are glossy black or brown, with orange or yellow legs or markings. Wings may be black with a blue sheen, orange or transparent. Males are usually smaller than females. *Tachypompilus ignitis* (length 47mm) shown. **BIOLOGY:** Female spider wasps run around rapidly, vibrating their wings and antennae and hunting spiders, which are paralysed and dragged back to a hole, where they are buried to provision the developing larvae. **HABITAT:** Common in most habitats, occasionally in gardens.

### Paper and potter wasps
Family Vespidae

**length 8–37mm** Diverse group of usually brown or yellow, narrow-waisted, social wasps. Colonies comprise reproductives and workers. Forewings fold along a longitudinal pleat when at rest. Includes potter wasps, which construct a round mud nest, and paper wasps, which construct paper nests.

### Brown paper wasps
*Belonogaster* spp.

**length 19–37mm** Usually brown, with a long, arched waist and dark brown wings. **BIOLOGY:** Construct papery, multicelled nests of wood pulp and saliva, usually suspended on a slender stalk. The young are fed chewed-up insects, usually caterpillars. These wasps defend their nests aggressively and can inflict a painful sting. **HABITAT:** Various habitats; they nest on plants, rock faces and buildings.

### Orange-tipped potter wasp
*Anterhynchium natalense*

**length 15mm** Potter wasps are distinguished by their long mandibles, which cross when closed, and by their solitary habits. **BIOLOGY:** *A. natalense* uses the disused nests of other potter wasps. Completed nests are provisioned with paralysed beetle larvae, spiders or caterpillars, and a single egg is laid in each. Adults feed on nectar. **HABITAT:** *A. natalense* is widespread in warmer parts of region, often collecting mud on puddle edges.

## Cockroach wasps
Family Ampulicidae

**length 3–33mm** Small to large, somewhat ant-like wasps with a pronounced neck-like constriction behind the head, longitudinal ridges on the thorax and usually metallic green or blue coloration, sometimes with red markings. Legs long and slender with tapering, drumstick-shaped femora. **BIOLOGY:** Best known for their unusual habit of provisioning nests exclusively with cockroaches. As the wasp is too small to carry the cockroach, the victim is lightly stung, then led by its antennae to the nest, where an egg is laid on its abdomen and the nest entrance sealed. **HABITAT:** Open woodland, but fairly rare.

## Mud daubers and sand wasps
Family Sphecidae

**length 1–40mm** 8 genera and >50 spp. in SA. Most are relatively large wasps with a narrow, elongate 'waist' known as a 'petiole'. Often brightly coloured, they construct mud nests or dig burrows and provision them with paralysed prey.

### Mud daubers
*Sceliphron* spp.

**length 17–27mm** Distinctively coloured, dull black wasps with long yellow waist, black legs with yellow bands, black antennae and clear wings. Female *S. spirifex* (length 17–27mm) shown. **BIOLOGY:** *S. spirifex* builds large, multicelled mud nests on walls, bridges or natural rock faces and provisions each nest with several spiders, before sealing the entrance with mud. Metallic blue false mud daubers of genus *Chalybion* are similar, but burrow in vertical banks. **HABITAT:** *S. spirifex* frequents cliffs, rocks and buildings throughout the region, especially in areas protected from rain.

### Thread-waisted wasps
*Ammophila* spp.

**length 19–29mm** Diverse genus of strikingly slender hunting wasps. Mostly black, with very long, slender waists; first half of the abdomen usually orange. Forelegs with comb-like sand rakes for digging; wings clear. **BIOLOGY:** Actively dig unbranched tunnels, which are provisioned with 1 large, or several smaller, caterpillars. May use pebbles to tamp down the sealed entrance to the nest. **HABITAT:** Ubiquitous, common on bare, sandy soil.

### Sand wasps and bee wolves
Family Crabronidae

**length 13–27mm** Diverse family of solitary, predatory wasps that provision their nests with paralysed prey. Sand wasps of the genus *Bembix* (shown, length 13–27mm) are typical: the abdomen has black-and-yellow or black-and-white bands, legs are yellow, wings are clear. Forelegs have large comb-like sand rakes. **BIOLOGY:** Excellent diggers; females excavate multicelled nests in sand and continuously provision them with flies as the larvae develop; they seal the hole only when the larvae reach maturity. **HABITAT:** *Bembix* spp. common in open, sandy areas, often close to the sea or along river banks.

### Membrane bees
Family Colletidae

**length 3–13mm** Common group of primitive, small to medium-sized, solitary bees that lack the pointed mouthparts typical of most bees. Usually dark-coloured, sometimes banded. Some have a brush of hairs on their hindtibiae for carrying pollen, as is typical for bees; others carry pollen in their crop. *Hylaeus heraldicus* (length 5mm) shown. **BIOLOGY:** Colletids nest in existing cavities or plant stems, lining the nest with transparent cellophane-like material – hence the family's common name. Larvae are fed on pollen and nectar. **HABITAT:** Common across the region in a variety of habitats.

### Sweat bees
Family Halictidae

**length 2–15mm** Diverse family of small to medium-sized, usually dark-coloured or metallic bees. *Nomioides* sp. (length 5mm) shown. **BIOLOGY:** Some are solitary; others social; multicelled nests are made in burrows in soil, wood or existing cavities and lined with a waxy material. All are pollen feeders; may be important pollinators. Some parasitize other bees, entering the brood cells of their hosts, eating the egg and laying another in its place. Often attracted to sweat, females can inflict a minor sting. **HABITAT:** Arid areas and open woodland throughout the region.

**SAWFLIES, WASPS, BEES AND ANTS**

## Leafcutter and mason bees
Family Megachilidae

**length 6–24mm** Mostly solitary bees, which have a brush of pollen-holding hairs under the abdomen, not on the hindlegs like those of other bees. Abdomen often black-and-white banded, or with black and yellow/orange sections. *Megachile combusta* (length 24mm) shown. **BIOLOGY:** Some nest in existing cavities, but many build nests in the open using either chewed or combed plant material (resembling cotton wool) or circular pieces cut from living leaves and petals. Nests typically comprise separate cells. Some species are 'cuckoos', laying eggs in the nests of other bee species. **HABITAT:** Common across the region in most vegetation types.

## Honey and carpenter bees
Family Apidae

**length 2–52mm** Large family, with >200 spp. in SA; comprises a diversity of bees, including carpenter bees, bumble bees, stingless bees and honeybees. Many representatives are hugely important pollinators in natural habitats and agriculture.

### Carpenter bee
*Xylocopa caffra*

**length 20–24mm** Large, stout bees that buzz loudly when flying. Sexually dimorphic: males entirely covered with yellow hairs, females (shown) black with 2 bands of yellow hairs across the rear of the thorax and abdomen. **BIOLOGY:** Territorial males patrol fixed areas around plants. Females excavate nest tunnels in dead wood, creating a series of brood cells separated by barriers of chewed wood, each stocked with pollen and nectar. One of about 36 spp. of carpenter bees in SA. **HABITAT:** Most habitats; nests in dead tree limbs.

### Honeybee
*Apis mellifera*

**length 13mm** Familiar, hairy, yellow-and-black social bee forming large colonies comprising a queen (the only fertile female), male drones and numerous sterile female workers. **BIOLOGY:** Nests comprise vertical combs with hexagonal cells lining both sides. Enormously important as pollinators of commercial crops and as a source of honey and beeswax. **HABITAT:** Builds nests in cavities in trees and cliffs, although now mostly found in artificial hives. Ubiquitous.

**SAWFLIES, WASPS, BEES AND ANTS**

## Ants
Family Formicidae

**length 1–40mm** Easily identified by the elbowed antennae and distinctive node-like structure forming the slender waist. Despite their global distribution, ecological dominance and enormous diversity, all 12,500 global species fall into this single family. (Termites, order Isoptera, p.24, although unrelated, are sometimes incorrectly called 'white ants'). All ant species are social, and colonies comprise well-differentiated castes of winged males or drones, female reproductives or queens (which discard their wings after mating) and sterile female workers and soldiers. Ants are of great economic significance: some play negative roles, damaging crops and invading buildings, delivering painful bites and toxic stings, or protecting aphids and other pests. Others play positive roles, such as aiding in seed dispersal and regulating insect pests.

### Red driver ant
*Dorylus helvolus*

**length 2–40 mm** Workers (length 2mm) are small, reddish brown with a square head and no eyes (bottom image). Soldiers (bottom image centre) are much larger, with a wide, rectangular head and large, pincer-like mandibles and bite vigorously. The winged males (top image, length 40mm) are huge, orange, bloated, cylindrical 'sausage flies' often attracted to lights. **BIOLOGY:** A predatory, nomadic species living in temporary subterranean nests and periodically moving to new locations in a long marching column defended by soldiers. **HABITAT:** Common in most habitats including urban settings and gardens.

### Harvester ant
*Messor capensis*

**length 5–12mm** Slow-moving, dark brown ant with large head and big globular abdomen. **BIOLOGY:** Form large nests in soil and gather grass seeds, carrying these back to the nest along well-worn pathways. Discarded seed husks form heaps around nest entrances. They assist in seed dispersal, since some seeds are dropped or left uneaten. Patches around nest sites have a higher nutrient and organic matter content and support different flora from the surroundings. **HABITAT:** Dry areas throughout the region; also found in gardens.

SAWFLIES, WASPS, BEES AND ANTS

### Black cocktail ant — *Crematogaster peringueyi*

**length 3–10mm** Small, black ant. Workers have a pointed, heart-shaped abdomen, held curved back over the thorax when alarmed (hence their common name). **BIOLOGY:** Best identified by their 'carton' nests made out of chewed vegetable fibres and built in elevated positions in trees and bushes. Workers tend aphids and other hemipterans for their honeydew and rapidly emerge to defend the nest if it is disturbed. Bites can be painful. One of several related species in the region, including reddish-brown *C. melanogaster* and red *C. castanea*. **HABITAT:** Coastal bush and trees.

### Fire ant — *Solenopsis punctaticeps*

**length 2–6mm** Small, dull orange-yellow ants, with a bulbous abdomen and clubbed tips to the antennae; workers may differ in size, the larger individuals having brown heads. **BIOLOGY:** Prey on termites and invade the colonies of other ants, feeding on their eggs and young. The larger, redder, invasive *S. geminata* is found in some urban areas and can inflict a painful sting. **HABITAT:** Colonies usually found under rocks and logs.

### Argentine ant — *Linepithema humile*

**length 2–3mm** Small, uniformly sized, plain brown ants, the waist being a single conical segment. **BIOLOGY:** They always run in trails. Form huge, diffuse colonies with many queens and spread by colony budding. An aggressive alien species imported with horse fodder during the Boer War. A significant pest, spoiling food, protecting aphids from parasites and predators and displacing the endemic ants that distribute and bury the seeds of fynbos plants. **HABITAT:** Diverse, but more common in disturbed sites, towns and farmland than in natural veld.

### Black sugar ant
*Lepisiota capensis*

**length 2–3mm** Small, jet black, diurnal ants with enlarged, swollen abdomen and paler legs and antennae. Last thoracic segment with 2 blunt spines. **BIOLOGY:** Pupate in cocoons. Easily confused with the alien invasive White-footed ant *Technomyrmex albicans*, which lacks thoracic spikes, is nocturnal and has naked pupae. **HABITAT:** Particularly common indoors in the Western Cape. Runs in trails; nests in walls, window frames and under pots.

### Spotted sugar ant
*Camponotus maculatus*

**length 20–25mm** Extremely large, yellow to reddish-brown ant with slender head and thorax, head and abdomen darker, the latter marked with yellow patches. **BIOLOGY:** Forages mostly at night, but does not run in trails. Workers do not sting, but tuck the abdomen under the thorax and spray attackers with formic acid. **HABITAT:** Live in small colonies of a few hundred under flat rocks throughout southern Africa.

### Bal-byter sugar ant
*Camponotus fulvopilosus*

**length 10–20mm** Among the largest, most familiar ants in SA; covered with golden hairs; has 3 black dorsal patches on the abdomen. Some workers and soldiers are big, with greatly enlarged heads. **BIOLOGY:** Do not run in trails, but forage individually in the heat of the day; alert and fast-running. Tend mealybugs for honeydew and prey on termites and other insects. Bites are painful; they can also spray formic acid some distance. **HABITAT:** Common in arid areas. Nest under large rocks.

### Pugnacious ant
*Anoplolepis custodiens*

**length 10–13mm** Large, reddish-brown ants with bands of silvery hairs on the abdomen. **BIOLOGY:** Colonies may have several queens. Workers are fast, aggressive, vary widely in size and approach intruders. Mostly predatory, but may tend aphids and pests, causing outbreaks. May prevent harvesting with aggressive biting. **HABITAT:** Large underground nests lack mounds around the entrance. Common in agricultural and natural habitats.

# GLOSSARY

**Abdomen** Last of the 3 major body divisions, after head and thorax.
**Arolium** Sucker-like structure situated between the tarsal claws.
**Blowfly strike** Infestation of living tissue by fly larvae, especially common beneath wool of sheep.
**Caste** A type of adult individual found in social insects, e.g. a worker or soldier.
**Cercus (pl. cerci)** One of 2 paired appendages at end of the abdomen.
**Colony budding** Expansion of a colony of social insects.
**Compound eye** Large lateral eyes of most insects, comprising numerous facets or lenses, each representing a separate visual unit, the ommatidium.
**Cosmopolitan** Widely distributed, found all over the planet.
**Coxa** First segment of the leg, where it joins the body.
**Crop** Enlarged foreregion of an insect gut, used for temporary food storage.
**Cross veins** Short veins on an insect wing that join longer veins and run parallel to the narrow axis of the wing.
**Dorsoventrally flattened** Flattened from top to bottom.
**Eyespot** Marking on an insect (often on the wing) resembling a vertebrate's eye.
**Fairy circles** Large, regularly spaced, circular bare patches in arid Namibian grasslands.
**Femur (pl. femora)** The third and, usually, largest segment of an insect leg (corresponds to the thigh in humans).
**Flange** Expanded ending of a structure.
**Forceps (of earwigs)** Enlarged and hardened cerci.
**Gall** A cancer-like growth on plants, caused by insects feeding.
**Head capsule** Part of the outer skeleton making up the insect head.
**Hemimetabolous** Undergoing incomplete metamorphosis, in that immatures resemble and gradually develop into the adult body form. Wing pads present in older nymphs.

**Holometabolous** Undergoing complete metamorphosis; life cycle comprises egg, larva, pupa and adult.
**Labial mask** Mouthparts in Odonata that cover the other mouthparts.
**Lachrymal fluid** Tear secretion from a vertebrate's eye.
**Mandibles** Paired 'jaws', or biting and chewing mouthparts (may be modified).
**Mesic** Areas with a reasonable amount of rainfall and vegetation ('wet' areas).
**Mesothorax** The middle of the 3 thoracic segments in an insect.
**Metathorax** The posterior of the 3 thoracic segments in an insect.
**Nama karoo** Very dry South African biome in the centre of the country.
**Nymph** Young stage of an insect that undergoes incomplete metamorphosis.
**Ootheca (pl. oothecae)** Hardened egg case containing developing eggs.
**Palps** Elongated sensory structures attached to insect mouthparts.
**Pheromone** Chemical released from the body of one insect to influence the behaviour or physiology of another, sometimes causing aggregation of individuals of the same species.
**Pronotum/pronotal shield** Shield-like plate covering the prothorax.
**Prothorax** The first of 3 parts of the insect thorax.
**Raptorial** Describes legs adapted for seizing and holding prey.
**Renosterveld** Vegetation found in the Western Cape that grows on shale soils.
**Reproductive/s** Describing the king and queen in social insects.
**Rostrum** The beak-like mouthparts of sucking insects.
**Scutellum** 'V'-shaped part of a bug's exoskeleton, at the end of the thorax.
**Simple veins** Veins in an insect wing that do not branch much.
**Soldier** Caste of social insects specialized for colony protection.
**Solitary phase** Stage in locusts' life cycle, where they do not form swarms.

**Suborder** A taxonomic group or division within an order.
**Succulent karoo** South African biome in the arid west, dominated by succulent plants.
**Swarming phase** Stage in life cycle of some insects where individuals group together and fly or walk in swarms.
**Tarsus** The last portion (= 'foot') of an insect leg, often consisting of 5 segments and ending in a pair of claws.
**Tegmina** Partially hardened forewings that protect the softer hindwings.
**Tibia** The fourth segment of an insect leg, between the femur and tarsus.
**Wing pads** Developing wings on the outside of the thorax in hemimetabolous insects.

# FURTHER READING

Picker, M., Griffiths, C. and Weaving, A. 2002. *Field Guide to Insects of South Africa.* Struik Publishers, Cape Town.

Woodhall, S. 2005. *Field Guide to Butterflies of South Africa.* Struik Publishers, Cape Town.

Tarboton, W.R. and Tarboton, M. 2015. *A Guide to the Dragonflies and Damselflies of South Africa.* Penguin Random House, Cape Town.

# INDEX TO SCIENTIFIC NAMES

**A**
*Acanthacris ruficornis* 40
*Acanthoplus armiventris* 34
Acanthostomatidae 51
*Acherontia atropos* 119
*Acmaeodera viridaenea* 75
*Acraea horta* 124
Acraeinae 124
*Acrida acuminata* 40
Acrididae 40
Acroceridae 95
*Acrotylus patruelis* 41
*Actenodia curtula* 82
Adelidae 108
*Aedes* 90
Aeolothripidae 61
*Aeropetes tulbaghia* 125
Aeschnidae 19
*Africallagma glaucum* 18
*Afroleptomydas* 94
*Afronurus harrisoni* 14
Aganainae 112
Agaonidae 131
Agaristidae 121
*Agoma trimenii* 121
Agromyzidae 101

*Aleurothrixus floccosus* 60
Aleyrodidae 60
*Allocnemis leucosticta* 18
*Alucita spicifera* 115
Alucitidae 115
Alydidae 49
*Amata cerbera* 112
*Amatonga* 37
*Amauris niavius* 123
*Amitermes hastatus* 26
*Ammophila* 135
Amphipsocidae 45
Ampulicidae 135
*Anaphe reticulata* 120
*Anax imperator* 19
*Anisops* 54
*Anoplolepis custodiens* 140
Anostostomatidae 32
*Anterhynchium natalense* 134
*Anthene definata* 129
*Anthia homoplatum* 67
  *maxillosa* 67
Anthicidae 81
*Anthomyia* 102
Anthomyiidae 102

Anthribidae 86
*Antliarhinus zamiae* 86
*Anurida maritima* 12
*Apate femoralis* 76
*Aphanicerca* 32
Aphididae 59
*Aphis nerii* 59
Apidae 137
*Apis mellifera* 137
*Aptera fusca* 23
Aradidae 48
ARCHAEOGNATHA 13
Arctiinae 111
*Argema mimosae* 117
Ascalaphidae 66
Asilidae 94
*Asota speciosa* 112
*Aspidomorpha puncticosta* 85
  *tecta* 85
*Astylus atromaculatus* 77
Athericidae 93
Athripsodes 106
*Atractocerus brevicornis* 77
*Australoechus hirtus* 96
*Austrophasma redelinghuysense* 43

Austrophasmatidae 43
*Azygophleps inclusa* 108

# B

Bacillidae 44
*Bactrodomena tiaratum* 44
Baetidae 14
*Baetis* 14
*Belenois aurota* 127
*Belonogaster* 134
Belostomatidae 54
*Bembix* 136
Berothidae 64
Berytidae 48
*Bibio* 91
Bibionidae 91
Bittacidae 88
*Bittacus* 88
Blaberidae 23
*Blattella germanica* 22
Blattellidae 22
Blattidae 21
BLATTODEA 21–23
*Blepharida* 85
Blepharoceridae 89
Bolboceratidae 70
*Bombomyia discoidea* 95
Bombyliidae 95
Bostrichidae 76
*Brachycerus omatus* 87
*Brachymeria kassalensis* 132
Braconidae 130
Bradyporidae 34
*Braula* 98
Braulidae 98
Brentidae 86
*Bromophila caffra* 98
Bruchidae 86
*Bullacris intermedia* 38

# C

Caenidae 15
*Caenis* 15
*Calidea dregii* 50
*Caliroa cerasi* 129
Calliphoridae 103
Calopterygidae 16
*Camponotus fulvopilosus* 140
*maculatus* 140
*Campylocera* 97
*Capitonisalda* 51
Carabidae 67
*Cassionympha cassius* 125
*Castanophlebia calida* 14
*Catharsius tricornutus* 74
Cecidomyiidae 92
*Cephonodes hylas* 120
Cerambycidae 83
*Cerapterus curtisi* 68
*Ceratitis rosa* 98
Ceratopogonidae 91
Cercopidae 58
*Ceriagron glabrum* 17
*Ceromitia turpisella* 108
*Ceroplastes destructor* 60
*Ceroplesis capensis* 83
  *thunbergii* 83
*Ceryx anthraciformes* 112
*Cestrotus* 100
*Chaematopsyche* 106
*Chaetonerius* 99
Chalcididae 132
*Chalybion* 135
*Chamanthedon* 110
*Charaxes jasius* 128
Charaxinae 128
*Charops* 130
*Cheilomenes lunata* 78
*Chiasmia simplicilinea* 115
*Chimarra ambulans* 107
Chironomidae 90
*Chironomus formosipennis* 90
*Chirotenon longimanus* 86
Chlorocyphidae 16
*Chlorolestes umbratus* 17
Chlorolestidae 17
Chrysididae 132
*Chrysis concinna* 132
Chrysomelidae 84
*Chrysomya chloropyga* 103
*Chrysoperla* 63
Chrysopidae 63
*Chrysoritis thysbe* 128
Cicadellidae 59
Cicadidae 58
*Cicindela quadriguttata* 68
Cicindelinae 68
*Cimex lectularius* 47
Cimicidae 47
Cixiidae 55
Cleridae 77
*Clogmia albipunctata* 89
*Clonia wahlbergi* 35
Coccidae 60
Coccinellidae 78
*Coeliades pisistratus* 123
*Coelopa* 100
Coelopidae 100
Coenagrionidae 17
*Coenobasis* 113
*Coenomorpha* 51
COLEOPTERA 66–87
COLLEMBOLA 12
Colletidae 136
*Colophon* 70
*Colotis danae* 126
*Comicus* 33
*Conchyloctenia punctata* 85
*Condylostylus makalaka* 96
Coniopterygidae 63
Conopidae 97
*Conops zonatus* 97
Coreidae 49
Corixidae 54
Corydalidae 62
*Corythucha ciliata* 47
Cossidae 108
Crabronidae 136
*Crematogaster castanea* 139
  *melanogaster* 139
  *peringueyi* 139
*Crocothemis sanguinolenta* 20
*Crombrugghia wahlbergi* 115
*Cryptochile assimilis* 80
*Cryptoflata unipunctata* 57
*Ctenocephalides felis* 105
*Ctenolepisma longicaudata* 13
*Culex* 90
Culicidae 90
Cupedidae 66
*Cupes capensis* 66
Curculionidae 87
*Cybister tripunctatus* 68

*Cydia pomonella* 108
Cydnidae 50
*Cyligramma latona* 122
*Cymatomera denticollis* 36
*Cythia cardui* 128

## D

Dactylopiidae 60
*Dactylopius opuntiae* 60
Danainae 123
*Danaus chrysippus* 124
*Dasineura dielsi* 92
*Dasypletis placodes* 94
Dejeania 104
Delphacidae 56
Derbidae 55
DERMAPTERA 30
*Dermestes maculatus* 76
Dermestidae 76
*Derocalymma* 23
*Deropeltis erythrocephala* 21
*Desmonemoura* 31
Diaspididae 60
*Dictyophara* 56
Dictyopharidae 56
*Dictyophorus spumans* 39
Diopsidae 99
*Diopsis* 99
*Diostrombus abdominalis* 55
DIPLURA 12
DIPTERA 89–104
*Dolicaon* 69
Dolichopodidae 96
*Dorylus helvolus* 138
Drosophiliidae 101
*Dysdercus* 49
Dytiscidae 68

## E

Ecclorolestes 17
*Echidnophaga gallinacea* 105
 larina 105
*Egybolis vaillantina* 122
Elateridae 75
*Eldana saccharina* 114
*Ellatoneura glauca* 17
*Elporia* 89

EMBIIDINA 42
EMBIOPTERA 42
*Emerus* 33
Empididae 96
*Empusa guttula* 29
Empusidae 29
*Encosternum delegorguei* 50
*Enicospilus* 130
EPHEMEROPTERA 14–15
*Ephestia* 114
Ephydridae 100
*Epilachna dregei* 78
Erebidae 111
*Eretmocera syleuta* 109
*Eristalis tenax* 97
*Esakiella hutchinsoni* 54
*Euboriella annulipes* 30
*Eupetochira xystopala* 110
Eupterotidae 118
Eurybrachidae 57
*Eurycorypha* 35
Euschmidtiidae 37
*Eutrichia capensis* 118
*Evania* 131
Evaniidae 131

## F

Flatidae 57
*Forficula senegalensis* 30
Forficulidae 30
Formicidae 138
*Formicomus caeruleus* 81
*Fucellia capensis* 102
Fulgoridae 56

## G

*Garreta nitens* 73
Gasterophilidae 104
Gasteruptiidae 131
*Gasteruption* 131
*Gedoelstia* 104
Gelastocoridae 53
*Geocnemis plagiata* 50
Geometridae 115
*Gerris swakopensis* 52
Gerridae 52
*Glossina* 102
Glossinidae 102
Gomphidae 18

*Gonocephalum simplex* 80
*Graphipterus trilineatus* 67
Gryllacrididae 33
Gryllidae 36
*Gryllotalpa africana* 37
Gryllotalpidae 37
*Gryllus bimaculatus* 36
*Gyponyx signifer* 77

## H

*Haematopota* 94
*Hagenomyia tristis* 65
Halictidae 136
*Harpagomantis tricolor* 27
*Harpezoneura multifurcata* 45
Hebridae 52
*Hebrus* 52
Hectopsyllidae 105
Heleomyzidae 100
*Helicoverpa armigera* 122
Hemerobiidae 63
HEMIPTERA 47–60
Hepialidae 107
Heptageniidae 14
*Hermetia illucens* 92
Hesperiidae 123
*Heteracris* 41
Heteronemiidae 44
*Heteronychus arator* 73
*Heterorachis devocata* 116
*Hetrodes pupus* 34
*Hilarempis* 96
*Hippobosca rufipes* 103
Hippoboscidae 103
*Hippodamia variegata* 78
*Hipporrhinus furvus* 87
*Hippotion celerio* 119
Histeridae 69
*Hodotermes mossambicus* 24
Hodotermitidae 24
*Holopterna alata* 49
*Hoplocoryphella grandis* 29
*Hyalites esebria* 124
*Hydrometra* 53
Hydrometridae 53
Hydrophilidae 69
*Hydrophilus* 69
Hydropsychidae 106

Hydrosalpingidae 107
*Hydrosalpinx sericca* 107
*Hylaeus heraldicus* 136
Hymenopodidae 26
HYMENOPTERA 129–140
*Hypolimnas misippus* 127
*Hypopholis sommeri* 72

### I

Ichneumonidae 130
*Ictinogomphus ferox* 18
*Imbrasia belina* 118
 *tyrrhea* 117
*Inxwala modesta* 55
*Ischnura senegalensis* 18
ISOPTERA 24–26
Issidae 56

### J

*Jana tantalus* 118
Japygidae 12
*Japyx* 12
*Johannesburgia* 56
*Julodis* 75
*Junonia archesia* 127

### K

*Karoophasma
 biedouwense* 43
*Kotochalia bunodi* 109

### L

*Labidura riparia* 30
Labiduridae 30
*Laccoris* 55
*Laccotrephes* 55
*Lacipa pulverea* 112
*Lamarkiana* 38
Lampyridae 76
*Laurhervasia setacea* 64
Lauxaniidae 100
*Lema daturaphila* 84
LEPIDOPTERA 107–129
*Lepisiota capensis* 140
Lepismatidae 13
Leptoceridae 106
Leptophlebiidae 14
Leptopodidae 51
*Leptosialis africana* 62

*Leptynoma sericea* 93
*Lestes* 16
Lestidae 16
*Lethocerus* 54
*Libanasidus vittatus* 33
Libellulidae 19
*Libyaspis wahlbergi* 50
*Ligariella* 28
Limacodidae 113
*Linepithema humile* 139
Liposcelidae 45
*Liposcelis bostrychophila*
 45
*Liriomyza* 101
*Locris areata* 58
 *arithmetica* 58
*Locustana pardalina* 40
*Lophyra brevicollis* 68
Lucanidae 70
*Lucilia sericata* 103
*Luciola* 76
Lycaenidae 128
Lycidae 76
*Lycus trabeatus* 76
Lygaeidae 49
Lymantriinae 112
Lymexylidae 77

### M

*Machiloides* 13
*Macroglossum trochilus*
 119
*Macrolister* 69
*Macrotermes natalensis* 25
*Macynia labiata* 44
Mantidae 27
Mantispidae 65
MANTODEA 26–29
MANTOPHASMATODEA
 43
*Maransis gramineus* 44
*Mausoleopsis amabilis* 71
MECOPTERA 88
*Megachile combusta* 137
Megachilidae 137
MEGALOPTERA 62
*Megaselia scalaris* 96
*Meinertellidae* 13
*Melanitis leda* 125
*Meloe angulatus* 82

Meloidae 82
Melyridae 77
Membracidae 58
*Menopon gallinae* 46
Menoponidae 46
*Meridiobolbus faustus* 70
*Mesa* 133
*Mesovelia vittigera* 52
Mesoveliidae 52
*Messor capensis* 138
*Metacanthus* 48
*Metallonotus aerugineus*
 81
*Microhodotermes viator* 24
*Micromus* 63
*Micronecta* 53
Micronectidae 53
Micropezidae 98
Milichiidae 102
*Mimegralla fuelleborni* 98
Miridae 47
*Mirperus jaculus* 49
*Monochelus
 niewoudtvillensis* 72
Mordellidae 82
*Mulvia albizona* 57
*Musca domestica* 102
Muscidae 102
*Mutilla astarte* 133
Mutillidae 133
Mydidae 94
*Mylabris oculata* 82
Myrmeleontidae 65

### N

*Narina* 48
Naucoridae 55
Neanuridae 12
*Neltumius arizonensis* 86
Nemestrinidae 95
Nemopteridae 64
*Neolophonotus* 95
*Neoperla* 31
*Nephrotoma* 89
Nepidae 55
Neriidae 99
*Nerthra grandicollis* 53
NEUROPTERA 63–66
*Neurosymploca* 111
*Nezara viridula* 51

Noctuidae 121
*Nomioides* 136
Notodontidae 120
Notonectidae 54
Notonemouridae 31
*Numicia insignis* 57
Nycteribiidae 103
Nymphalidae 123
Nymphalinae 127

## O

*Ochtera* 100
Ochteridae 53
*Ochterus caffer* 53
ODONATA 16–20
*Odontotermes badius* 25
*Oecanthus* 36
Oecophoridae 110
*Oedaleus* 42
*Oenopia cinctella* 78
Oestridae 104
*Oligotoma saundersii* 42
*Omorgus asperulatus* 70
*Oncopeltus famelaris* 49
*Onitis alexis* 73
*Onosandrus* 32
*Orthoctha dasycnemis* 41
ORTHOPTERA 32–42
*Oryctes boas* 73
*Oxyrachis* 58

## P

*Pachnoda sinuata* 71
*Pachylomera femoralis* 74
*Palmipenna aeoleoptera* 64
*Palpares caffer* 65
*Palpita unionalis* 114
*Palpopleura jucunda* 20
Pamphagidae 38
*Pantala flavescens* 20
*Papilio dardanus* 126
  *demodocus* 126
Papilionidae 126
*Paratoxapoda* 99
*Paropioxys jacundus* 57
*Passalidius fortipes* 67
Paussidae 68
Pediculidae 46
*Pediculus humanus capitis* 46
*Pencillidia fulvida* 103
Pentatomidae 51
*Periplaneta americana* 21
*Perkinsiella saccharicida* 56
Perlidae 31
*Phalera imitata* 120
*Phanerotoma bertolonii* 79
*Phaon irridipennis* 16
PHASMATODEA 44
*Philematium natalense* 84
*Philoliche rostrata* 94
Philopotamidae 107
Phlaeothripidae 61
*Phoracantha recurva* 83
  *semipunctata* 83
Phoridae 96
PHTHIRAPTERA 46
*Phyllocrania paradoxica* 26
*Phymateus viridipes* 39
Phymatidae 48
Pieridae 126
*Pingasa* 116
*Piophila casei* 101
Piophilidae 101
Plataspidae 50
Platycnemidae 18
*Platycypha caligata* 16
*Platypleura* 58
Platystomatidae 98
PLECOPTERA 31–32
*Plecia ruficollis* 91
Pleidae 54
*Plutella xylostella* 113
Plutellidae 113
Pneumoridae 38
*Podallea* 64
*Poecilocarda cosmopolita* 59
Polymitarcyidae 15
*Polyspilota aeruginosa* 28
Pompilidae 134
*Pontia helice* 127
*Popa undata* 29
*Porphyronota hebreae* 72
*Povilla adusta* 15
*Promeces longipes* 84
*Prosoeca* 95
*Prosopistoma* 15
Prosopistomatidae 15
Protoneuridae 17
*Psammodes striatus* 79
*Psammotermes allocerus* 25
Psephenidae 74
*Pseudagrion* 17
*Pseudoclimaciella* 65
*Pseudocreobotra wahlbergii* 27
Pseudophyllodromiidae 23
*Psilodera fasciata* 95
Psocidae 45
PSOCOPTERA 45
*Psococerastis* 45
Psychidae 109
Psychodidae 89
Psychopsidae 66
Psyllidae 59
Pteromalidae 132
Pterophoridae 115
Pthiridae 46
*Pthiris pubis* 46
*Ptyelus grossus* 58
Pucilidae 105
Pyralidae 114
*Pyrgomantis rhodesica* 28
Pyrgomorphidae 39
Pyrgotidae 97
Pyrrhocoridae 49

## R

Reduviidae 48
*Retroacizzia mopanei* 59
Rhagionidae 93
*Rhagovelia* 52
Rhaphidophoridae 34
*Rhigioglossa* 93
*Rhinocoris* 48
Rhinotermitidae 25
Rhipiceridae 70
*Rhodogastria amasis* 111
Ricaniidae 57

## S

Saldidae 51
*Saltoblattella montistabularis* 22
*Sarcophaga pachtyli* 104
Sarcophagidae 104
Saturniidae 117
Satyrinae 125

Scarabaeidae 71
*Scathophaga stercoraria* 101
Scathophagidae 101
*Sceliphron spirifex* 135
*Scelophysa trimeni* 72
*Schiffermuelleria pedicata* 110
*Schistocerca gregaria* 41
Schizodactylidae 33
Sciaridae 92
*Sciobius* 87
Sciomyzidae 99
*Scolia wahlbergii* 133
Scoliidae 133
Scutelleridae 50
Scythrididae 109
*Separaspis capensis* 60
*Sepodon* 99
Sepsidae 99
Sesiidae 110
*Sia pallidus* 33
Sialidae 62
*Sigara* 54
Silphidae 69
*Silveira jordani* 66
Simuliidae 91
SIPHONAPTERA 105–106
*Sirex noctilio* 130
Siricidae 130
*Sisyphys* 74
*Sitophilus oryzae* 87
*Solenopsis punctaticeps* 139
*Speleiacris tabulae* 34
Sphecidae 135
Sphingidae 119
*Sphingomorpha chlorea* 122
*Sphingonotus scabriculus* 42
*Sphodromantis gastrica* 27
*Spialia* 123
*Spodoptera littoralis* 121
Staphylinidae 69
*Stenocara* 80
*Stenotus* 47
Stenopelmatidae 33
*Sternocera orissa* 75
Stratiomyiidae 92

STREPSIPTERA 88
*Strigocoris* 48
*Strongylium purpuripenne* 81
Stylopidae 88
*Suilla picta* 100
*Supella dimidiata* 23
*Synhoria testacea* 83
Synlestidae 17
Syrphidae 97

## T
Tabanidae 93
Tachinidae 104
*Tachypompilus ignitis* 134
*Taeniochauliodes ochraceopennis* 62
*Tagoropsis flavinata* 117
*Tarachodes* 28
*Technomyrmex albicans* 140
*Temnopteryx phalerata* 22
*Tenebrio molitor* 81
Tenebrionidae 79
Tenthredinidae 129
Tephritidae 98
Termitidae 25
Tessaratomidae 50
*Tetiella* 37
*Tetralobus flabellicornis* 75
Tetrigidae 37
Tettigoniidae 35
*Thanatophilus mutilatus* 69
Thaumetopoeidae 120
Thripidae 61
*Thrips tabaci* 61
*Thyretes caffra* 113
Thyretidae 113
THYSANOPTERA 61
THYSANURA 13
*Tinea pellionella* 109
Tineidae 109
Tingidae 47
Tiphiidae 133
Tipulidae 89
*Tithoes confinis* 84
*Tmesibasis lacerata* 66
Tortricidae 108
*Trachypetrella* 38

*Trichacantha atranupta* 93
*Trichilogaster acaciaelongifoliae* 132
*Trichoplusia orichalcea* 121
TRICHOPTERA 106–107
*Trichostetha fascicularis* 71
Tricorythidae 15
*Tricorythus* 15
Tridactylidae 37
*Tridactylus* 37
*Trinervitermes* 26
*Trioza erytreae* 59
Triozidae 59
*Trithemis arteriosa* 19
 *furva* 20
Trogidae 70
Tropiduchidae 57
*Tunga penetrans* 106

## U
*Utetheisa pulchella* 111

## V
*Valleriola moesta* 51
Veliidae 52
*Venus leto* 107
Vespidae 134
*Viridiphasma clanwilliamense* 43

## X
*Xenos* 88
*Xya* 37
*Xylocopa caffra* 137
Xyloryctidae 110

## Y
*Yponomeuta fumigata* 110
Yponomeutidae 110

## Z
*Zabalius aridus* 35
*Zanna* 56
*Zaprionus* 101
*Zerenopsis lepida* 116
*Zonocerus elegans* 39
*Zophosis testudinaria* 79
*Zosteraeschna minuscula* 19
Zygaenidae 111

# INDEX TO COMMON NAMES

## A
Acraea, Dusky 124
  Garden 124
Acraeas 124
ALDERFLIES 62
ANT(S) 129–140
  Argentine 139
  Bal-byter sugar 140
  Black cocktail 139
  Black sugar 140
  Fire 139
  Harvester 138
  Pugnacious 140
  Red driver 138
  Spotted sugar 140
  White-footed 140
ANTLION(S) 63–66
  Gregarious 65
  Mottled veld 65
Aphids 59

## B
Backswimmers 54
  Pygmy 54
Bagnet, Reticulate 120
Bagworm(s) 109
  Wattle 109
Barklice, Common 45
BEE(S) 129–140
  Carpenter 137
  Honey- 137
  Leafcutter 137
  Mason 137
  Membrane 136
  Sweat 136
BEETLE(S) 66–87
  African black 73
  Ant 81
  Ants' nest 68
  Blister 82
  Blue monkey 72
  Bronze dung 73
  Brush jewel 75
  Burrowing ground 67
  Carcass 70
  Carpenter bee blister 83
  Carrion 69
  Chequered 77
  Cicada parasite 70
  Click 75
  CMR 82
  Common tiger 68
  Darkling 79
  Dor 70
  Dune tortoise 85
  Dusty maize 80
  Emerald tiger 68
  Flattened giant dung 74
  Flea 85
  Fool's gold 85
  Frantic tortoise 79
  Giant jewel 75
  Glittering jewel 75
  Green dung 73
  Green protea 71
  Ground 67
  Hide 76
  Hister 69
  Ladybird 78
  Large barred monkey 72
  Leaf 84
  Long-legged ground 80
  Longhorn 83
  Metallic tree darkling 81
  Net-winged 76
  Oil 82
  Predaceous diving 68
  Red-banded blister 82
  Reticulated 66
  Rhinoceros 73
  Rove 69
  Royal tree darkling 81
  Scarab 71
  Ship-timber 77
  Soft-winged flower 77
  Spider dung 74
  Spotted tortoise 85
  Stag 70
  Streaked ground 80
  Three-horned dung 74
  Tiger 68
  Tumbling flower 82
  Two-spotted ground 67
  Tyrant ground 67
  Velvet ground 67
  Water scavenger 69
Blackflies 91
Bloodworms 90
Blowfly/flies 103
  Banded 103
  Copper-tailed 103
Bluebottles 103
Blues 128
Bluet, Swamp 18
Bluetail, March 18
Boatmen, Pygmy water 53
  Water 54
Bollworm, Army 122
BOOKLICE 45
Booklouse, Domestic 45
Borer(s), Auger 76
  Eldana 114
  Eucalyptus 83
  Sugar-cane 114
Botflies 104
  Horse 104
BRISTLETAILS 13
  Rock 13
Brown(s), Evening 125
  Rainforest 125
  Twilight 125
Brush-foots 127
Bufftip, Imitating 120
BUG(S) 47–60
  Ambush 48
  Assassin 48
  Bark 48
  Bed 47
  Broad-headed 49
  Burrowing 50
  Capsid 47
  Cochineal 60
  False stink 51
  Flat 48
  Giant water 54
  Inflated stink 50
  Lace 47
  Lantern 56
  Leaf-footed 49
  Long-winged snout 55
  Milkweed 49
  Moth 57
  Pill 50
  Plant 47

Primitive snout 55
Rain-tree 58
Red-spotted spittle 58
Saucer 55
Seed 49
Shield 51
Shield-backed 50
Shore 51
Snout 56
Spiny shore 51
Spittle 58
Stilt 48
Stink 51
Toad 53
Velvet water 52
Velvety shore 53
Burnets 111
  Belted 111
Burrowers, Pale 15
BUTTERFLY/FLIES 107–129
  Brush-footed 123
  Milkweed 123

## C

CADDISFLIES 106–107
  Finger-net 107
  Golden horn 107
  Long-horned 106
  Web-spinning 106
Caenids 15
Chafer, Garden fruit 71
  Marbled fruit 72
  Rose 72
  White-spotted fruit 71
Charaxes 128
Cicadas 58
Clear-wings, White-banded 110
Clegs 93, 94
Clubtails 18
Cochineal insects 60
COCKROACH(ES) 21–23
  American 21
  Banded 23
  Bark 23
  Blaberid 23
  Blattellid 22
  Cape zebra 22
  Common 21
  German 22

Pseudophyllodromid 23
  Red-headed 21
  Table Mountain 23
Coppers 128
Cotton stainers, 49
Craneflies 89
Crawlers, Stout 15
Cream-striped Owl 122
CRICKET(S) 32–42
  Armoured ground 34
  Barred king 32
  Bush 35
  Camel 34
  Common garden 36
  Dune 33
  Green Corn 34
  Grey Corn 34
  Jerusalem 33
  King 32
  King 33
  Leaf-rolling 33
  Mole 37
  Pygmy mole 37
  Tree 36
  Water 52
Cycad looper 116

## D

Damsel(s), Common pond 17
  Pond 17
DAMSELFLIES 16–18
Daubers, Mud 135
Demoiselle(s) 16
  Glistening 16
Diadem 127
DIPLURANS 12
  Japygid 12
DOBSONFLIES 62
DRAGONFLY/FLIES 18–20
  Gold-tail 18
Dropwing, Dark 20
  Navy 20
  Red-veined 19
Dusters 116

## E

EARWIG(S) 30
  Common 30
  Long-horned 30

Ring-legged 30
  Striped 30
Emerald, Red-lined 116
Emperor, Blue 19
  Gold-marbled 117
  Willow 117
  Zigzag 117
Ermine, Speckled 110

## F

Featherlegs 18
Fireflies 76
FLEA(S) 105–106
  Cat 105
  Chigoe 106
  Common 105
  Hen 105
  Jigger 105, 106
  Sticktight 105
FLY/FLIES 89–104
  Banana stalk 99
  Bat 103
  Bat louse 103
  Bee 95
  Big-headed 97
  Black scavenger 99
  Bristly robber 94
  Cattle louse 103
  Coffin 96
  Common coffin 96
  Common house 102
  Dance 96
  Drone 97
  Dung 101
  Flesh 104
  Fruit 98
  Fruit beetle parasite 97
  Golden bee 96
  House 102
  Hover 97
  Jackal 102
  Kelp 100
  Lauxaniid 100
  Leaf-mining 101
  Long-legged 96
  Louse 103
  March 91
  Mydas 94
  Natal fruit 98
  Needle-nose 94

**INDEX TO COMMON NAMES**    **149**

Robber 94
Root-maggot 102
Scuttle 96
Seaweed 100
Shore 100
Signal 98
Small-headed 95
Snail-killing 99
Snipe 93
Soldier 92
Stalk-eyed 99
Stilt-legged 98
Sun 100
Tachinid 104
Tangle-veined 95
Tsetse 102
Vinegar 101
Warble 104
Water snipe 93
White-tipped bee 95
White-tufted robber 95
Wormlion 93
Footman, Crimson-speckled 111
Foresters 111
Friar 123

## G
Gallfly, Acacia 92
Glider, Wandering 20
Glowworms 76
Gnats 90
 Dark-winged fungus 92
Goat, Leopard 108
Golden Plusia 121
GRASSHOPPER(S) 32–42
 Bladder 38
 Burrowing 41
 Canary 41
 Common redleg 41
 Common stick 40
 Elegant 39
 Foam 39
 Koppie foam 39
 Lubber 39
 Short-horned 40
 Stone 38
Greenbottles 103
Groundhoppers 37

## H
Hairtail, Common 129
Handmaidens 111
HANGINGFLIES 88
Hawk, Oriental bee 120
Hawker(s) 19
 Friendly 19
HEELWALKER(S) 43
 Fynbos 43
 Green 43
 Namaqualand 43
 Southern 43
Honeybee 137
Hoppers, Bush 37
Horntails 130
Horseflies 93
 Green-eyed 93

## I
Inspector, Garden 127

## J
Jewel (s) 16
 Dancing 16
Jigger 106

## K
KATYDID(S) 32–42
 Bark 36
 Large leaf 35
 Oblong-eyed leaf 35
 Winged predatory 35

## L
Lacebug, Sycamore tree 47
LACEWING(S) 63–66
 Beaded 64
 Brown 63
 Dusty-winged 63
 Green 63
 Rock spoonwing 64
 Silky 66
 Spoonwing 64
 Threadwing 64
Ladybird(s), Black-ringed 78
 Herbivorous 78
 Lunate 78
 Spotted amber 78
Lappet, Cape 118
Leafhoppers 59
Leafworm, Cotton 121
Leaproach, 22
LICE 46
 Bee 98
 Biting bird 46
 Crab 46
 Human 46
 Pubic 46
LOCUST(S) 32–42
 Brown 40
 Desert 41
 Garden 40
 Green milkweed 39
 Rain 38
 Shield-backed 38
 Short-horned 40
Longhorn, Common metallic 84
 Dusted 108
 Giant 84
 Large green 84
 Pondo-pondo 83

## M
Maiden, Bar 113
 Heady 112
 Yellow-sleeved 112
Malachites 17
MANTID(S) 26–29
 Common green 27
 Eye-flower 27
 Flower 27
 Grass 28
 Large grass 29
 Leaf 26
 Marbled 28
 Stick 29
 Bark 28
 Common 27
 Flower 26
 Gargoyle 29
 Ground 28
Mantidflies 65
Mantispids 65
MAYFLIES 14–15
 Flathead 14
 Prong-gilled 14
 Small minnow 14

**INDEX TO COMMON NAMES**

Mealworm, Yellow 81
Midges 90
  Biting 91
  Gall 92
  Net-winged 89
Monarchs 123
  African 124
Mosquitoes 90
  Bush 90
  House 90
MOTH(S) 107–129
  African hummingbird hawk 119
  African maiden 113
  African maiden 113
  Carpenter 108
  Case-bearing clothes 109
  Clear-wing 110
  Clothes 109
  Coddling 108
  Concealer 110
  Death's-head hawk 119
  Diamond-backed 113
  Diamond-backed 113
  Dried fruit 114
  Eggar 118
  Emperor 117
  Ermine 110
  Flower 109
  Forester 121
  Geometrid 115
  Ghost 107
  Giant lappet 118
  Goat 108
  Grassland 110
  Grassland 110
  Gypsy 112
  Hawk 119
  Lappet 118
  Longhorn 108
  Luna 117
  Many-plume 115
  Monkey 118
  Moon 117
  Mopane 118
  Orange plume 115
  Owlet 121
  Peach 122
  Plume 115
  Powdered gypsy 112
  Processionary 120
  Puss 120
  Pyralid snout 114
  Silver-spotted ghost 107
  Silver-striped hawk 119
  Slug 113
  Specious tiger 112
  Sphinx 119
  Sundowner 122
  Swift 107
  Tiger 111
  Tomato 121
Mothflies 89

## O

Oblique Peacock 115
Opal, Common 128
Owl flies 66

## P

Painted Lady 128
Parktown prawn 32, 33
Plant lice, Jumping 59
  Triozid 59
Planthoppers, Delphacid 56
  Dictyopharid 56
  Eurybrachid 57
  Issid 56
  Ricaniid 57
  Tropiduchid 57
Pond skaters 52
Prominents 120
PSOCIDS 45
  Hairy 45
Psylla, African citrus 59
Psyllid, Blue gum 59

## R

Rollers, Leaf 108

## S

Sandmen 123
SAWFLIES 129–140
Scale insects, Armoured 60
  Soft 60
Scale, Aloe red 60
Scarlet, Little 20
SCORPION FLIES 88
SILVERFISH 13
  Domestic 13
Skimmers 19
Skipper(s) 123
  Cheese 101
Slug, Pear 129
  Tobacco 84
Specs, Water 15
Spreadwings 16
SPRINGTAILS 12
  Pudgy 12
Squaregills 15
STICK INSECT(S) 44
  Bacillid 44
  Giant 44
  Grass 44
  Thunberg's 44
STONEFLIES 31–32
  Cape 32
  Porcupine 31
  Southern 31
  True 31
Sulphurs 126
Swallowtail(s) 126
  Citrus 126
  Mocker 126

## T

Table Mountain Beauty 125
TERMITE(S) 24–26
  Black-mound 26
  Common fungus-growing 25
  Harvester 24
  Higher 25
  Large fungus-growing 25
  Northern harvester 24
  Sand 25
  Snouted harvester 26
  Southern harvester 24
  Subterranean 25
Threadtail(s) 17
  Grey 17
THRIPS 61
  Banded 61
  Common 61
  Tube-tailed 61
Tiger(s), Snouted 112
  Tri-coloured 111
  Trimen's false 121
Tigertail, Common 18

Tip(s), Orange 126
  Scarlet 126
Toktokkie, Spindle 79
  Striped 79
Treehoppers 58
Twig-wilters 49
TWISTED WING
  PARASITES 88
Two-pip Policeman 123

## V
Velvet ants 133

## W
Walking sticks, Common 44
WASP(S) 129–140
  Acacia gall 132
  Braconid 130
  Brown paper 134
  Carrot 131
  Chalcidid 132
  Cockroach 135
  Common fungus-growing 25
  Cuckoo 132
  Ensign 131
  Fig 131
  Harvester 24
  Higher 25
  Ichneumon 130
  Large fungus-growing 25
  Mammoth 133
  Northern harvester 24
  Orange-tipped potter 134
  Paper 134
  Potter 134
  Pteromalid 132
  Sand 135, 136
  Sand 25
  Spider 134
  Subterranean 25
  Thread-waisted 135
  Tiphiid 133
Water measurers 53
Water pennies 74
Water scorpions 55
Water-treaders 52
WEBSPINNERS 42
  Saunders' 42
Weevil(s), Bean 86
  Common 87
  Cycad 86
  Fungus 86
  Maize 87
  One-spot fungus 86
  Pea 86
  Primitive 86
  Prong-tailed 87
  Red-spotted lily 87
  Rice 87
  Snout 87
White, Brown-veined 127
  Meadow 127
White Pearl 114
Whitefly/flies 60
  Woolly 60
Whites 126
Widow, Yellow-veined 20
Wing(s), Blue 42
  Yellow 42
Wolves, Bee 136
Woodwasp(s) 130
  Sirex 130